LOVE

is

OUT THERE

TRUE STORIES OF  Hope FOR SINGLE WOMEN OVER 30

MELISSA WILLIAMS POPE

Busy Quill Books

Published by Busy Quill Books
For more information please email: info@thebusyquill.com

ISBN 978-0-473-31977-9

To my precious girlfriends, near and far, who are "this close" to giving up hope of ever finding love.

And to Shane, who proved that my hope was not in vain.

Acknowledgments

First, I would like to thank the ladies around the world who took the time to share their hearts and their love stories for this project. I believe God chose you to be a part of this and I look forward to many testimonies of hope from the readers!

Thank you to my family who instilled in me the belief that I could do anything I set my mind to, including publish books, which meant I was able to take my place on the starting block of this project without doubt.

To my precious girlfriends who've journeyed the single road with me, and I with them: thank you. Your love and encouragement through the years has been invaluable. And to the ones who are still single and waiting, it was your beautiful faces in my mind that kept me running the race to get this book out.

Thank you, Shane, for your love, help and unwavering support, especially when it felt like I was clawing my way across the finish line.

Finally, thank you, God. I'm incredibly humbled that You have entrusted me with this important and special project and I'm so grateful that You allowed me the opportunity to have a story of my own to include within its pages.

Table of Contents

Introduction

"Once you choose hope, anything is possible."
- Christopher Reeve

The Beauty of Testimony

"And they overcame . . . by the word of their testimony,"
(Revelation 12:11 NKJV).

Testimonies are powerful! They build our hunger for miraculous possibilities. Whatever the breakthrough; be it healing, debt cancelation or salvation, hearing the stories of others gives us faith to claim the same things for ourselves and our loved ones. If God did it for them, He can surely do it for us!

This is why I've compiled stories of real women around the world who have walked the path you're walking now. Not all of them would consider themselves great writers, but they each share a passionate desire to encourage you by recounting their journeys. I like to see these as letters from a mixture of favourite aunts and close girlfriends, sharing their hearts.

They, like you, have waited. At times trudging through disappointment, anger and unbelief, and at times, blanketed in hope, trust and peace. Some lived in remote country towns (where men were scarce), or were lost in the big city. Some believed they "did everything right," (so where's my man?) and still others felt they had "made messes of their lives." But each of them uniquely experienced God's faithfulness as they saw the fulfillment of their long held desire for marriage.

You won't find "smug marrieds" giving pat answers that annoy you, but rather women who've cried out to God for a perfect-for-them husband, and whose testimonies will give you a hope infusion to keep holding on and believing that God will give you your heart's desire, too.

How to Use This Book on Your Journey

I know that some of you may never have actually prayed, either for yourself regarding this topic, or for your future husband. In the *What's Next* chapter at the end of this book, I've included two sample prayers to get you started.

I've also included a 21-Day Heart Exploration Experience with questions that are perfect for your private journaling and prayer times. You might also consider creating your own *Love is Out There* Heart Exploration group to go through this book and the 21-Day Experience with your friends. You'll be amazed at the difference surrounding yourself with supportive girls on the same journey can make!

Why This Book?

While bouncing between countries a couple of years ago, the idea came to me.

A friend had just married and I was SO happy for her! SO happy because I knew she had waited for a loooooong time for God to bring her new husband to her. And I remembered years ago, when she was in her mid 30's, how she talked about making peace with her singleness and going through a raw, painful journey of trusting God with it. At the time, mid 30's was ages away for me and I admired this serenity and wisdom she had about everything.

One night at a party, I did some subtle fishing with a guy one of my friends really liked only to make a sad discovery. He wasn't interested in her. There were tears in my eyes for her on the way home. And I prayed. But I was also a bit annoyed. She was an awesome girl! So many friends longed for that special someone. WHERE. Was. He?!

A new mission was born. I started to pray with and for my girlfriends regarding our future husbands. And declare that they were on their way, dang it; in Jesus' name, these guys were on their way!

Back to a couple of years ago when that one friend got married. It was like a spark of hope had ignited. If it can happen for her, then it can happen for others. And if it can happen for others then . . . it can happen for me.

After all, I'm in my 30's now. And it's become my story, too.

And so I thought that I would create this inspirational book and compile a nice big handful of these hope-sparking stories. I was so excited about this idea, I hardly slept for a couple of days. Yet I didn't feel any peace to move forward. Argh. Don't you hate when it's clear that the Holy Spirit is putting something on hold when you're just chomping at the bit!

So I guess I just sort of forgot about it.

Until a year later, all of a sudden, out of nowhere, quite unexpectedly, this book project came to mind again. And I knew it was the right time to start my search for stories.

But what I didn't know was that I was about to meet *my* future husband that very week and end up with a story of my own!

So, beautiful one, if you feel like you've waited until you can't wait any longer, if despondency and doubt are setting in like a mist on the moors, let these stories be a rope to hoist you out of that swamp of despair.

Believing with you,
Melissa

> *"Those who sow in tears shall reap*
> *in joy. (She) who continually goes forth*
> *weeping, Bearing seed for sowing, Shall*
> *doubtless come again with rejoicing,*
> *Bringing (her) sheaves with (her)."*
> *Psalm 146:5-6 NKJV*

Katie's Story

"Family and friends were worried I would remain in that 'simply awful state': Single."

Like every young girl created, I dreamed of the day my knight would come and rescue me from all my distresses and make my life perfect. He would be my hero, my defender, my protector, my provider, my lover and my friend. Just like out of a BBC period drama.

I'd only had one boyfriend by the time I met my first husband at a Christian camp. I was 18 and he was 20. He was artistic, sanguine, Tigger-ish and I know I followed him around with googly eyes, just enthralled with all the art and culture he introduced to me. A year later, we attended the same college and we were best of friends. When we graduated, he went his way into teaching and I went back home to be with my family after my father died. We wrote letters continuously, spent Christmases together and called each other often.

I loved him from the start, but it took him a while to come around to my way of thinking. We married in 1994 when I was 24. And immediately, something wasn't right. It's kind of obvious now, but I was so sheltered and naïve that I didn't understand what was going on. Three months into our marriage, he told me he was gay. Another year passed as we sought counseling, even deliverance to fix our marriage. One move and three months later, he left. Eight months after that, our marriage was annulled as it had never been consummated. We were married for only 22 months.

To say that I was devastated would be an understatement. To say that I distrusted men and felt like I could exist well enough without them . . . well, that was my announcement to well-meaning family and friends who were intent upon seeing me "fulfilled in marriage."

A few years went by and I healed. I was happy and LOVED being single. God brought me to a place of utter contentment in him. He truly was "my Ishi" – my Husband (Hosea 2) and I was irritated when people said I "needed a man." To me, God was enough. And truly, He is ALWAYS enough. I loved being single! I loved the journey of just me and God.

At that time, I was living in the least populated county east of the Mississippi River – 2,500 people in the county. No stoplights. No McDonald's. No Wal-mart. And not a whole lot of great choices in the eligible bachelor category. I was 31 and family and friends were worried I would remain in that simply awful state: "single." I wasn't looking but I had told the Lord that if I was ever to marry again, I wanted . . . and I gave Him my list. I remember specifically telling Him, "and for my cherry on top, I would love someone with a British accent." I left Him with that conversation and went on with my life.

On November 11, 1996 (I know because it's written in the margin of the page), I was having some quiet time and the Lord led me to Isaiah 46:11: "From the east I summon a bird of prey, from a far-off land, a man to fulfill my purpose. What I have said, that I will bring about; what I have planned, that I will do." (NIV). When I read that, it hit me SO hard, I felt like I'd been slammed across a room. See, you gotta know me. I'm an "all things English" nut. BBC, tea and scones, Downton Abbey, Fry,

Laurie, Jane Austen – I'm SO there! I even do a great British accent.

I dreamed of going to my heart country one day, but that was like dreaming of flying to the moon. A lovely thought, but not likely to ever happen. But when I read that verse, the "far country," "from the east," suddenly read as "husband from England." Call me crazy; I sure did. As did my pastor ("don't get your hopes up") and some others who were convinced I was dreaming myself into a BBC fantasy. But I thought, "God, surely . . .surely . . . if anyone can do it, YOU can. But really? This is just me being weird or stupid. So, if it's You, confirm it." I would say that to God over the next five years: "If it's You, confirm it." In fact, I said it so many times and asked for confirmation, and then re-confirmation, and confirmation of the re-confirmation!

You know when people say they want something "written in the clouds"? I wasn't trying to not believe; I was just trying to make sure that this time around, I really DID hear from God. I mean, I thought I had the first time. I'm sure it was fear-driven, this need for confirmation. I REALLY didn't want to screw up again. I didn't want to miss God and HIS choice for me. Never once did I feel that God was frustrated or disapproving. He ALWAYS confirmed.

And He even confirmed when I wasn't asking, through many ways. I even got my cloud confirmation. Driving down the highway one day with friends, praying inside and saying once again, "God, really. Once again, are You sure? Is this REALLY you? A husband from England? Please. Just one more time. Tell me again." At that moment, I looked out my window to my right, and a lorry drove right past me. On the side of the truck:

"ENGLAND" and a coat of arms. I stopped asking for confirmation after that. I figured God had spoken and couldn't make it any plainer.

Meanwhile, since that November, I was praying for my husband. I had no idea who he was, where he was, what he looked like, what his life was like. But I prayed. There is no distance in the Spirit of God. It didn't matter if I was a whole world away (in the least populated county). I prayed. I prayed for his job, for his walk with God, for his family, for his parents (my future in-laws), for his dogs (if he had them), for his church, for his health. Whatever I might pray for him if I knew him in person, I prayed for him unseen. And, at times, I prayed for myself. Lord knows, we both needed it.

Those well-meaning friends and family? Like Job's friends – "you need to not trust God"? "You need to join a single's club. You need to drive to the Valley (an hour one way) and find friends and get married." I ignored them. I figured if God had me in this sparse place and He hadn't released me to leave, then He would either bring my husband to me or He would release me to leave when it was time.

In the summer of 2001, our church contacted some friends who oversaw the mission trips for college students at Brownsville School of Ministry, in Florida. We asked for students to come help us run our yearly children's camp outreach, and a team of 15 signed up. I was scheduled to host two of the gals on the team and on the evening of their arrival, I was waiting at the door for them. When I opened my door, the two girls were there, along with a tall fella who was carrying their luggage. We said a brief "hello" and then he dropped the bags and returned to the car where the other team members were waiting to continue on to their host houses.

An hour or so later, the phone rang and our pastor invited us over for an impromptu prayer meeting in the barn with the team. The gals and I got ready and we rode over to the pastor's house. There was a whole lot of hustle and bustle going on when we got there, but this was usual for them. I came in and saw this guy sitting at the table, the same one I briefly met on my doorstep. I didn't pay much attention until I heard him speak. He had an accent. It was British. I grabbed the pastor's son and said "Who is that?" He started smiling and said, "That's Chris. He's from England." I thought, "No! NOOO!!! This didn't just happen. Not in front of all these people!"

It wasn't that I mentally rushed to an altar. I just knew the looks and smiles and pointed gazes that would be occurring over the next two weeks while the team was there. Turns out, it wasn't all that bad. I did have trouble concentrating at the prayer meeting that night. Couldn't pray at all. Until I grabbed a girl and said, "Pray for me! I can't pray." She laughed. Like she knew something I didn't.

Two weeks later, the team was packing up to leave and return to Florida. But as the pastor had really taken a liking to Chris – both of them being very scholarly, and the pastor's son was leaving in two more weeks for the same college, he invited Chris to stay on and ride down with them later. During that time, Chris would come into my office (I was our church's administrator / secretary) and sit and argue points of the Bible with me. I didn't like him much, but there was something about him . . . And then, of course, there was that accent.

In mid-August, the night before Chris left for Florida, I said goodbye to him and told him I'd see him again. He said, "I'll never be back here. I'm not called to these mountains." I don't know what it was but I KNEW he'd be back. Didn't know why, but he'd be back.

The next few weeks were horrible. I couldn't eat. I couldn't sleep. I couldn't concentrate. I wasn't in love; I mean, I liked the guy but I wasn't crazy about him. I just couldn't stop thinking about him. And missing him. But I wasn't in love (wink, wink). When the pastor called from Florida and told me that they were bringing Chris back to Virginia with them, so he could do his internship at our church, I was relieved. And not surprised. My pastor was my spiritual father and I know he was angling to get his "daughter" married.

Chris came back to the mountains and showed up in my office early September. He was rooming at my pastor's house (which incidentally was just down the road from my apartment) so we were together a lot of the time.

He came over for dinner one night a few weeks later, and had "THE Talk." You know, the one . . . "I have feelings for you. I don't want to date. If you have feelings for me, then we are talking about marriage." I cried. I was thrilled. I was scared. But I wasn't confused. I knew. I knew it was God.

I knew it was God when he said he'd gotten saved in August, 1996 that I had started praying for him in November, 1996. I knew it was God that the missions director at the college had been my old landlord (and one who had walked beside me through the loss of my first spouse) and friend and had spent 17 hours on the drive from Florida to Virginia telling Chris about this "church secretary who . . ."

I knew it was God when three months later, we said "I do" on December 31, 2001. And I've known it was God these past ten years, when this "man of My purpose" has been used by God to do a work in my heart, my life, bring healing, sharpen, shape and mold.

Has it always been easy? No. Has it always been perfect? No. Do we struggle in our marriage? Yes. But ONLY God could have done this. And there are lots of details and things I've left out. But ONLY God could have brought my husband "from the east" "from a far country" via Florida to Virginia to land on my very doorstep in the least populated county east of the Mississippi River. God delivered His perfectly planned gift to me, personally, all the way from England. And He even gave me my very "cherry on top."

My advice to any single girl is this: Fall in love with Jesus. Seek Him. Let Him become your everything, your Ishi, your husband. Tell the Lord what you would like or think you need in a mate, and then leave it with Him. Then pray for that person. If you are 30 years old, that fella is out there now, going to work every day, experiencing joys and trials. He doesn't just pop into existence when he appears in your life. So pray for him now. Listen to the Lord for him. If you would do so when you get married, start now. And trust that your Father hears and sees and He will do what is best for you, and your future mate.

Katie Patrick
Port Huron, Michigan, USA

*"I was praying for my husband. I had no idea
who he was, where he was, what he looked like,
what his life was like. But I prayed."*

Tami's Story

"What ever happened to, 'He will give
me the desires of my heart'?
Aren't I owed that?"

"Tami, if I asked you to be single for me, would you?" I
felt the nudge of the Lord once again. Could it be? Could
God really be asking me that question? What ever
happened to, "He will give me the desires of my heart"?
Aren't I owed that? At the time I was 37 years old, never
married, and yes, I thought God owed me that.

Ugh. I wish I could tell you I handled that well. I sure
didn't. I kicked, screamed and yes – did the ugly cry. For
several weeks, I put a brave face on publicly but oh I
cried buckets privately.

Having walked with the Lord for about five years, I was
embarrassed about how badly that affected me. "I'll do
anything for you, Lord!" "My life is yours, Jesus!" All
great "spiritual words" until He takes you up on them and
then you realize they were just words. If I was really as
spiritually mature as I thought I was . . . instead of kicking
my feet, I would have said, "Yes, sir." Everything
changes when God takes us out of the classroom and out
on a field trip.

Knowing I had tasted and seen for myself how good the
Lord was, I knew turning back was not an option for me. I
spoke to a Pastor at my church who said two things to me.
"God is asking if you would, not I am calling you to,"
and, "If you don't trust God with this, Tami, you will

never be prepared for the next thing He asks you to trust Him with." I listened. I felt defeated but I listened.

I got up the next morning, reality hanging on me like a noose, and realized I had to completely depend on God to walk this out. I knelt at my bed and began to pray for God to help me accept this bitter drink of sacrifice. As soon as I knelt down I felt so ashamed that I couldn't remember the last time I had knelt before my Lord. Remembering this now, still stings my eyes with tears. I was a head-strong, self-sufficient leader who had forgotten just how much she needed her Savior. Almost as instantly as I felt shame, a rush of peace swept over me and I began to be ministered to by the Holy Spirit. I knew that God was in all of this and I needed to walk it out . . . wherever it may lead.

I began to pour myself into ministry at my church. I was the volunteer leader of our Singles Group. You know that saying, "serve others and your trials get smaller"? It's true. It's very true. God met me in my loneliness as I served others. I honestly began to accept a life of singleness. God was faithful to encourage me when I needed encouragement. He gave me everything I needed to get through each day. Guess what? I began to build a life as a sold out single for God. Crazy, huh?

Over the next year, the Lord began to show my Pastor a call on my life for full-time ministry. In 2005, I left an 18 year career to join the staff of Connection Church as Connection Director. The advice I had received a year prior, "If you don't trust God with this, Tami, you will never be prepared for the next thing He asks you to trust Him with," rang the bell of truth in my heart. The move of leaving my career was very easy because God had already built a foundation of trust with me. He is such a good Father.

Fast forward six years, I felt the Lord prompt (more like shake my shoulders) to take a study called Changes That Heal by Henry Cloud. I can't recommend this to anyone (especially those single over the age of 30) enough. Other than the word of God, no other book has come close to changing my life. During the course of this study, I began to understand some of my behaviors and why I thought the way I did. It was truly life changing. I began to do the hard work of not only self-examination but put into practice what I learned. God began changing me into an open – connected person.

Soon after completing that study, I felt a stirring in my heart of wanting to be married. My view of marriage completely different now. I no longer looked for someone to complete me and be a little god for me by filling in the gaps. Jesus completes me. I wasn't looking for a soul mate, I was looking for someone to run my race of faith together with. That's not just Christian chatter; I deeply, deeply believed that to be true. When we seek God wholeheartedly, things change. A more factual statement would be . . . we change. God is so stinkin' smart. What I initially considered to be a season of loss, God was using it to prune and prepare my life for what He had for me.

The big theme of Changes That Heal is taking responsibility for your life. And the notion of getting out there making myself available to meet Christian men was something I knew I needed to do. I put myself out there, but didn't meet anyone. One day when I was praying, I asked God *how* to pray about this. I felt I had done the hard work to get ready for "something" or "someone" and nothing was happening.

I was directed to this scripture, "I say to myself, 'The LORD is my portion; therefore I will wait for him.'" (Lamentations 3:24 NIV). Each and every time I felt dissatisfaction rise up in me, I quickly spoke that scripture out loud and those thoughts were taken captive. Again, have I told you lately how smart God is?

On a whim I joined Christian Mingle, not expecting much to happen, but thought I'd try it. In April 2011, I met a great man named Cal Walker. We began dating and over time fell in love. Cal is a committed Christian who, in addition to deeply loving Jesus, has love and laughter as his calling card. It doesn't get much better than Cal. Did I mention he is romantic, writing me poetry and often brushes my hair? Worth the wait?! I would have gladly waited another 20 years to meet him.

In March 2012, on a snowy evening walking around Milford, Michigan, Cal took my hands in his, dropped to one knee and said these words, "You've made me so happy, I will never leave you, I will never raise a hand against you and I want to live with you the rest of my life. Will you marry me?"

On August 3, 2014 just one week shy of my 45th birthday, a never married, single woman became Mrs. Cal Walker. We believe, our union, without doubt, was orchestrated by God. Faith in God means having faith in His timing. An honest observation is this: had we met in 2004 when I so desperately wanted to be married Cal wouldn't have been interested in me. I had a rough edge to me that he wouldn't have been drawn to. (Enter the pruning process – yes, God is such a good Father.) When we met we were very compatible both in our walks with God, and how we live and love in every day life. Life is good and we are blessed.

I've walked that lonely road, girlfriend. I know the tears
you cry when no one is around or the thought, "Is he the
one?" that races through your mind each time you meet an
eligible man. I lived it, I get it.

I want to leave you with some encouragement and bacon.
Because you know everything goes better with bacon.
During my long single season, I went through a fast food
drive-thru to grab a quick bite to eat. In my head I was
screaming, "I want a burger with bacon and gooey sauce,
that's what I want!" But in reality I ordered the healthiest
choice, a grilled chicken wrap. Hmmph! When I opened
my bag I couldn't believe what met my eyes. Not one, but
TWO angus beef, cheese, bacon, gooey sauce wraps. It
took my breath away and scared me for a second. And
then I quickly came to my senses and ate . . . BOTH!

The story in the story is this . . . Psalm 84:11 tells us "For
the Lord God is a sun and shield; the Lord bestows favor
and honor. No good thing does he withhold from those
whose walk is blameless." (NIV). Sweet friend, if God
cares enough about giving this girl some bacon; don't you
think if marriage is a good thing for you it will happen? I
do.

I don't believe every single person will be married, but I
believe most can be. If the Lord feels that it's in your best
interest, that it's a good thing, I believe it will happen.
One of the greatest gifts God has given me was the
prompting to take full advantage of my single years. In
my singleness season, I tackled my issues from childhood,
reduced my financial debt substantially, paid attention to
my health and lost weight. Not to mention sought the
Lord wholeheartedly and watched Him change me from

the inside out. He didn't waste a day. God is trustworthy and He is faithful.

Tami Walker
Canton, Michigan, USA
www.cggirls.org

> *"God was faithful to encourage me when I needed encouragement. He gave me everything I needed to get through each day."*

Sue's Story

*"It's not like there's a long list of guys knocking
on my door and I'm turning them down.
The men are nowhere to be seen!"*

When I was living abroad in the United States during my
college years, it usually surprised me to hear that many of
my friends had had their first kiss while they were still in
elementary school. For me, I had hoped and prayed that I
would only share my first kiss with my future husband.

I know it sounds naïve and perhaps idealistic. I guess I
heard many stories from friends, as well as read plenty of
books, and made a decision that physical intimacy was
something special I wanted to share with only one person.

That one person didn't show up till I was at the ripe "old"
age of 31. By that time, I had received countless well-
meaning pieces of advice on how to meet men, how I
should be content with singlehood for this season in my
life, or how I should not have such high expectations. I'm
sure you have heard at least one of these things as a
single. I agreed with most of the advice given to me,
except maybe the part of having expectations that were
too high. My response to that was always, "It's not like
there's a long list of guys knocking on my door and I'm
turning them down. The men are nowhere to be seen!"

However, I did agree with my late dad that I would never
meet someone sitting at home, but more likely at a (young
adults) party. So I did make efforts to hang out in groups
where there were single men. At the very least, I could
practice my communication skills with them. I also did

enjoy my singlehood and took the opportunity to travel to Europe, read plenty of books, volunteer on a mission ship and serve at my local church. I wasn't sitting at home pining for my life to start. I was living life to the fullest!

However, that is not to say I did not desire to meet a guy and be married. It was my heart's desire and it came up in many conversations. There were days where I wondered if there were any good guys above 30 still single. And sometimes people would say things that seemed to imply I wasn't good enough or wasn't trying hard enough, (i.e. not forward enough). I didn't believe in asking men out – I believed that if the guy was interested, he would ask me out! But God is good and he put friends alongside me who encouraged me, spoke truth into my life, and assured me to keep focused on God. I repeatedly released my desires to God, knowing that He loved me and whatever the outcome, His plans for me were always good.

I met my husband Jonathan at the most unlikely of places – Hard Rock Café. I say unlikely because it isn't/wasn't our "style" to hang out at a venue like Hard Rock, and in fact, it was my first time there. For this one God-ordained moment, we were both there attending a singles inter-church event, along with a hundred other singles. For me, I had chosen to go after much persuasion (i.e. force) from a pastor at church, and because I knew my late dad would have wanted me to go.

You see, my dad often worried about my lack of suitors. He tried to set me up a few times, to no avail; and he also asked me to consider organising an inter-church singles event to widen my network and increase the chances of meeting "the one." He even promised to fund my efforts. I laughed at his idea because, "wouldn't that just seem too desperate?"

So when I heard about this event, just eight months after his sudden passing, I knew that if he were alive, there would be no question that he would have paid and signed me up the moment he got word of it. What more, the event was held on Father's Day – another reason why I could not not go. I'd like to believe that this was no coincidence.

Jon was a 35-year-old God-fearing man. As a family man at heart, he was beginning to wonder when he would be able to settle down. He was actively serving in his church, and had a great career going for him. He attended the event with little expectations, and went only to accompany his cell group leader, who happily paid for his ticket.

Kudos to our church leaders who organised this inter-church "Rocking Singles" event that allowed Jon and I to meet. They had a genuine heart to see young people find godly life partners within the church – or at the very least, to meet more fellow believers and build solid friendships. They reminded us on that day, to just have fun and forget the pressure of meeting "the one" at the event. With the group games they organised, they were successful in getting us to do just that.

When it was time for the meal, we were asked to ensure that each table had a representative from the different churches, and at least one guy. Yes, there was a shortage of guys, not surprisingly. To be exact, there was one guy to every three girls in attendance. That's how I met Jon. He was already seated at the table with another girl, and I plonked myself at his table, not because I had my eye on him or because he stood out from the rest, but because it was awkward to be wandering around looking for an empty seat!

After the initial introductions, Jon and I found out that we had mutual friends. Much to my surprise, he remembered seeing me at a friend's wedding two years ago. Together with the other girl at our table, we talked about ministry, work and hobbies – nothing earth-shattering!

During the meal, I could see the other girl losing interest in the conversation. (After the event, she jokingly remarked that Jon seemed interested in me. But I told her I didn't think so.) There were some other activities thereafter, which split the three of us till the end of the event. On my way out of Hard Rock, I bumped into Jon and we just said a casual "bye," and that was it. I didn't expect to see him again. But I did two weeks later.

I will share this – sparks at the first meeting aren't everything. I wasn't attracted to Jon until our third date. It was only after I had gotten to know him better, that I knew I wanted to be more than just friends. I say that to caution some readers who write men off that fail to impress at the first meeting. Give it time, some of us aren't as quick to reveal our true selves.

Once it was clear that we were both interested in moving further on in the relationship, Jon was very intentional in telling me that he was looking for a relationship that led to marriage, nothing else. That didn't scare me at all. In fact, I appreciated his honesty because I wasn't looking for a fun night out either.

Since I had always wanted to marry my first boyfriend, I made sure that before agreeing to be his girlfriend, I would at least be 90% sure that he was the one to marry. I say 90% because I don't think we ever know 100%. Part of the decision is faith, and trust in God because we do not control our futures. I did not know for sure that we would end up married, but I trusted that if we were both dating intentionally, and there were no red flags, our relationship would end in marriage.

Early in our courtship, I told Jon that I wanted us to save our first kiss for our wedding day, and sex was obviously a big no-no. He agreed. Unfortunately we did not wait to share our first kiss on our wedding day – we did however kiss only after we were engaged.

Meeting your husband in your 30s definitely has its advantages and disadvantages. For me, the advantage was that we were both more mature (I'd hope) and stable in life. We had our own interests and we were clear on what we wanted in a life partner. I'm honestly not sure if I would have been ready for a relationship in my 20s as I had much to learn about myself. We were also more realistic, rather than idealistic, in our expectations for marriage – it wasn't going to be a bed of roses all the time!

Do I sometimes wish I met Jon in my 20s? Yes. I wish I started dating him earlier because being single for so long also meant I was too independent and I didn't have the habit of sharing my time and energy with someone. It also meant that I don't have the luxury of time in waiting to have kids.

Jon and I had, to me, a rather long engagement – just over a year. It was our heart's desire, and perhaps impatience, to be married six months into our engagement. In fact, we hurriedly set a date and announced it our family; only to later be told by Jon's father, that he wished us to delay our wedding to the next year. You might cry foul and think, why? Believe you me, we were devastated too.

Jon's younger brother had also just gotten engaged and
his dad wanted for our weddings to be far apart enough
that we each got the attention we deserved. His father also
wanted to get to know me better. After all, Jon and I had
only known each other for 5 months before we were
engaged. We protested that, we cried, but in the end we
conceded. We were still single and God designed fathers
to be the head of the family, so we chose to honor his
father's wisdom in the matter.

Jon and I were married on 25th January of 2014, when I
was 32 going on 33, and he, 36 going on 37. Our friends
and family were of course thrilled for us – "finally!" they
all exclaimed. In hindsight, we are glad that we heeded
Jon's father's advice. The longer engagement not allowed
only me to get to know his family better, but it also gave
Jon and me more time to learn more about each other and
grow as a couple.

We spent time ironing out our differences during our premarital counselling sessions (not all of them obviously);
and we gave our full attention to Jon's brother's wedding,
and shared fully in his joy. In the end, God knew that we
needed more time. What's more, the initial date we chose,
ended up to be a terrible date, as Kuala Lumpur was
shrouded in haze and our semi-outdoor wedding would
have been a bust!

I'm so thankful for how and when Jon came into my life.
Marriage is a gift, and so is singlehood. No doubt there
were seasons in my life that I wondered if I would ever
get married and if God had something good in store for
me. But deep down inside I knew and trusted that no
matter what happened, God loved me and wanted the best
for me. And if marriage was it, He would want to give it

to me. And if singlehood was it, then He would give me the grace to accept it.

To all the readers, I say, don't lose hope. Trust in God. He wants the best for you and will give you more than you ever hoped for.

Chew Sue Lee
Kuala Lumpur, Malaysia

> *"Deep down inside I knew and trusted that no matter what happened, God loved me and wanted the best for me."*

Kelly's Story

"I dated so many frogs, I was definitely
wondering if there was anyone left for me."

It was my 30th birthday and I was at the top of Oxo Tower in London, sipping cocktails and looking out as the sun set over the bustling city. Whilst I was not exactly where I thought I'd be (married at 24, 2.5 kids and a white picket fence), I hadn't sat back and moped. I was living the dream, having moved to the UK, and was making the most of working and travelling in Europe during my single season.

This was a fabulous date (only our third) and more was to come that evening; a stolen kiss, dinner at Covent Garden, tickets to the Lion King and a rickshaw ride to a funky jazz club. Only it all came to a shattering end when the so-called Christian guy leaned over and whispered in my ear, asking if I would come back to his hotel.

"God, where is my Prince Charming?!" I cried, "I've waited all this time . . . is there no one left for me?" I climbed onto the old double decker night bus alone to ride home disappointed and disillusioned, not sure if I would ever find my one true love. Ten days later my visa to stay in the country got declined on technicalities and everything was about to change.

Five and a half years later, I sit here with one hand on my blooming belly, sipping my chai latte and smiling at my gorgeous husband, thanking God for declined visas, small towns and for the "frogs" I met along the way.

Who would have thought my Prince Charming was not in London with its population in excess of 8 million, but instead, back in my homeland, in the little beachside town of Orewa, New Zealand, and that just two and a half years after coming home, we would promise our hearts to each other forever, and Blair would whisper in front of all our family and friends that I would always be his Princess.

Whilst I am not the age of most Cinderellas or even the modern day romcom heroines, ours has been a fairytale story. I found my happily ever after.

Don't get me wrong, I'm not saying everything is perfect and that there won't be any struggles, just that my husband is perfect for me. As I said in my vows, "in (him) I have all I need, I know my prayers have been answered and all of my dreams have come true . . . you were truly worth the wait."

So how did it all start? TradeMe! No, I wasn't dating online (although some of my now married friends met this way so I'm not knocking that at all), I was looking for a flatmate or if worst came to worst, a flat to move into (and TradeMe is a New Zealand website for people to buy/sell/find jobs or accommodation, much like Gumtree or Craigslist in other parts of the world).

After a series of interviews with some "interesting" people, a message popped up on my screen, "Two Christian guys looking for another Christian guy to flat with." I thought what the heck, I'll give it a go; maybe they'll take a Christian girl instead. Plus, a lovely lady encouraged me saying, "They might have friends!" Little did I know that while I was typing my reply, these two guys were praying. Blair was a student at Bible College and with an empty room he was down to the last of his savings. As he says, I would be the answer to his prayers, in more ways than one.

God knows our hearts and just what we need. When I moved in, both of us were completely blind to the other. We didn't think of each other as anything more than flatmates, giving us the time to get to know each other without masks or pretense, and to have fun and build a trust that would later be foundational.

I do remember the day though (a week after I had said I was moving out for a job down in Auckland), that Blair gave me the "look." Not a flatmate glance, but an up and down check out look; I just about had kittens. Suddenly he was planning walks for us to take and I knew something had changed.

One evening at Wenderholm Regional Park, I tested my theory and sure enough, the walk turned into a run, a little flick of water and then into a full on water fight, after which he held my hand for the first time. The next day when I prayed, "My flatmate, God, really?!" I felt His gentle prompting and reply, "Check your list." Yes – I had a list. Not superficial stuff but detailed things that mattered to me. I wanted him to be practical so he could fix things like my dad AND bright (preferably with a degree, as silly as it sounds). I wanted someone on the same page as me, plus much, much more.

That year I had begun to question if maybe I was being "too picky," as some people said. After all, if my family friend had called me a spinster at 26 years old, how would I be viewed now?! Thankfully Papa God knew my fears and at small group earlier in the year, my leader prayed for me, not knowing my ponderings that week, and he specifically said that he felt God was saying not to give up or settle for second best. So here I was, hanging on to God's promises.

As I checked my list, my eyes got wider and wider; Blair loved God passionately - tick, loved his family - tick, that week I had just found out that not only was Blair at Bible College but he already had a degree in Recreational Management, was a qualified electrician and had won the national title of Apprentice of the Year, so bright and practical – tick, tick. In fact, he was the first person to tick every box on the list. Freak out time. Now what do I do?!

That night, I opened my "Word For Today" devotional booklet which happened to be on Ruth (how appropriate). It specifically said not to say anything, to prepare yourself and wait, just as Ruth had done, adorning perfume and resting at Boaz's feet. Talk about specific instructions! On one hand this wasn't easy for an assertive chick, but on the other, I am a firm believer that the guy needs to be the one to pursue (after all, it's in their DNA). Plus, I had asked God what to do and here it was in black and white.

So I waited . . . and waited . . . Blair held my hand on several more occasions and we talked for hours at a time, but he said nothing about "us." And still I waited (okay it was only two weeks but it felt like an eternity). Friends with benefits are a no go! But poor Blair was tying himself up in knots trying to figure out if I actually liked him. He was wondering, did I do this with all the boys (I could have shot him when he later told me that one – it wasn't like I had even dated anyone for the 9 months we flatted together!), was he was reading this situation correctly and what if he stuffed this up? But he finally got up the courage to tell me how he felt. And as they say, the rest is history.

Blair prayed that he would be blindsided by the girl that he fell in love with and that they would be friends first. He had no idea how it would be answered, but one day he found his prayer answered with a flatmate who ultimately became his "blindside" and his bride. In his words, the key was to keep praying. God's timing is perfect. He knows each of us intimately and knows the journey both people need to take. And His creativity in answering prayer is infinite – He made the universe and everything in it, what can't He do for you?

One of the good things about being older was that we both knew what we wanted. Within a week of "going out" we were talking about marriage. We both knew this wasn't some casual fling. However, I wasn't prepared for it when Blair suggested we should get married within 6 months.

My mother had a history of three failed marriages and I had believed that I my university boyfriend of 3 years would be my forever, so would need a few God signs this time. I was also fairly certain that any relationship needed to stand the test of time before wedding bells should ring (two years minimum to make sure there weren't too many dark and dirty secrets lurking in the closet).

But God has a great sense of humour. After a few intense conversations with my best friend (someone I consider wise and in tune with God), I realised that I was not my mum, this was the person I wanted to spend the rest of my life with and that the time spent flatting together as friends had in fact given me greater insight into his character then any amount of dating would. Plus, I already knew that we could live together (even in our old age and set ways) and not kill each other! With that realisation, came a real sense of peace. I still wanted a few more God signs though and they were on their way.

For the next month, we heard story after story of people who had met and been married within a super short amount time. People that never dated and just got engaged, people that just knew, weddings within three months, and all these people were still happily married 20, 30, 40 years on. We hadn't told anyone of our thoughts, the stories just came out of the woodwork from people we'd known, new folks we met and they just didn't stop. It was a surreal and exciting time; God was preparing us and what a journey we were on. As I was moving to Auckland and starting a new job, Blair decided that maybe I needed a bit more time to cope with all the changes, but he didn't wait too long. Less than three months later, he popped the big question.

Saturday the 12th of March, 2011, in true fairytale style, Blair planned and orchestrated the most amazing night. Dinner at Iguacu (a gorgeous restaurant in Auckland with food to die for and twinkling fairy-lights galore), hot tubs over a pit of burning coals surrounded by candles under a moonlit sky and finally, three thousand Dahlias in the shape of a heart on the beach where everything had first began. I forgot to mention that I am a true romantic; this was something at the bottom of my list. BIG TICK. This was a night to remember and our wedding would be just the same. On December 10th 2011, I married my Prince Charming.

One final thing, a little side note and hopefully encouragement. I use to laugh at this joke, "Why are men like parking spaces? All the good ones are taken." From my experience it was true! I dated so many frogs, I was definitely wondering if there was anyone left for me. The answer was YES! The perfect one, just for me.

More amazingly, Blair had only ever had one girlfriend, had never kissed anyone before me and we had both saved ourselves for our future spouse, waiting until our wedding night. So it can be done, we didn't regret it, in fact thank God for it and have felt so blessed along the way.

Don't expect the Hollywood movie, but know that the journey is better - you get to learn together, grow together in a safe and real relationship and you don't have all the baggage. God wants the best for us, don't settle for anything less. God has given me an Ephesians 3:17-21 love story, more than I could ask or hope for, and my prayer is that you will wait and trust him to deliver the same for you.

Kelly Vercoe
Tauranga, New Zealand

"Whilst I am not the age of most Cinderellas,
I found my happily ever after."

Bobbie's Story

*"I was nearly 55 and hadn't dated
since everything fell apart. I couldn't.
Surgery had left me feeling hideous."*

"This is for my brother, Butch. He'd love it here."

My Christian friend and traveling companion, Terry, was snapping photos over the heads of the congregation.

I was horrified. You would never take pictures in a synagogue during the worship. I had only come here, to a Jerusalem church, because she had graciously come with me to Jewish worship at a synagogue the previous Friday night.

I had come to Israel looking for something. Five years of breast cancer and associated health problems had led to the breakdown of my marriage and the failure of my business. I was nearly 55 and hadn't dated since everything fell apart. I couldn't. Surgery had left me feeling hideous.

I had been alone for the last two years. It was time to pick myself up again. I wanted some purpose and meaning to my life. Israel would be the place for a Jew to look, I thought. I never expected to find what I was seeking in a Christian place of worship. And, yet, straight off, I experienced the warmth of the people and the praise in that auditorium. This grew into a powerful electricity running through me that I now recognize as the Holy Spirit.

At the end of the service, I remained in my seat, stunned. I had not wanted to come and now I didn't want to leave. I hoped with all my heart that Terry would be willing to go on with me to the 24/7 Prayer Tower we'd just been invited up to.

Right now, she was quietly reviewing her photographs beside me, with a bewildered look on her face.

The man in front of us, putting on his coat, said, "There were angels here tonight."

Terry's eyes were like saucers.

"There were angels here tonight, Bobbie," she told me. "They're in my camera!"

She held it out.

The first picture was of a military tank we saw in the Jaffa Road, ahead of coming in. The second, taken here, was something else entirely. None of the things she'd pointed her camera at as she tried to capture the feel of this place for her brother, Butch, were there.

There was only a swathe of buttery gold, with a thick ridge running through the center, like the vein of a feather, close up. The next shot was like a progression from the first, only now what looked like tongues of golden flame danced their way across it.

Puzzled, I looked around for some point of connection between the pictures and our surroundings. There was none.

By the fourth shot in the sequence, the auditorium, streaked with purple, was showing through. By the fifth, it was as if the weird pictures had never been.

Of course they could have been the result of a glitch in Terry's camera. Yet, inside my head, a little voice was saying that everything about tonight had been unexpected and unprecedented and, okay, yes, supernatural. Was it beyond belief that the waves of love that had felt so real I wanted to reach out and grasp them had been captured and manifested in these pictures?

I would have left it at that, even so. Terry didn't. She spent our last day in Israel on a quest for their meaning. When she returned to our guest house, late in the afternoon, her face was white and shining. She had been told by a messianic rabbi — a rabbi who believed in Jesus — that something big would happen. And there was a rug, she said, a Persian picture rug.

"We're both on it, riding horses."

Later that night, she told me, "You're an integral part of this."

I had no idea what "this" was.

I was back in my native UK when the people she'd met sent the rug to her Canadian home. The pictures she sent me amazed me. There were four riders, two male and two female. The females looked like us.

I had to go and see the rug for myself.

I had never been to Eastern Canada, where Terry now lived. She and I had met more than twenty years before, when she was living Out West. She had done all the visiting in recent years, when I was sick.

It had been a long time since I'd traveled long haul.

After a flight to Halifax, Nova Scotia, the next stage of my journey was by very slow train to Moncton, New Brunswick. The conductor, imposing in dark uniform and cap, checked my ticket and said, "Would you like to be the Able-Bodied Savior?"

Being the Able-Bodied Savior sounded pretty wonderful. I said, "Yes."

He led me to the train doors at the end of the compartment and went through the emergency evacuation procedure. So that was it! I nodded and grinned as he showed me everything.

"So now it's official," he said, leading me back to my seat. "You are the Able-Bodied Savior."

He stuck a yellow post-it note on the luggage rack, above my head. After he left, I jumped up to read it. Sure enough, it said: Able-Bodied Savior.

I remembered what Terry had said as we talked on the phone, the previous week. "I get the strongest feeling that God wants to show you something on your way here."

He just had. I was definitely that person. I had a yellow post-it note to prove it.

Terry's house was deep in rural Canada, surrounded by deer and rabbits, just like the deer and rabbits on the rug.

Terry and I stood with a bunch of her friends she'd invited to meet me, staring at the rug. It was hanging in the upstairs hallway, opposite my bedroom door.

"It's you guys, for sure, both of you!" one said.

The others agreed.

"What's it all about?" another wanted to know.

"I don't know," I said, a little rueful. I had spent a lot of my visit here gazing at it, but nothing new had come to me.

We decided to visit Terry's brother, Butch — the one she'd snapped photos for at the worship in Jerusalem. He lived in Fredericton, which was many miles away. Everything was.

Three times, we tried to get there. The first time, her vehicle broke down in the middle of nowhere and her husband had to come rescue us. The second, a tropical rainstorm was falling from the skies. On our third try, we made it.

There was an instant chemistry between us. After two years in the wilderness, ducking all advances, a whiff of chemistry was worth its weight in gold. I returned from that cup of tea meeting to write in my diary that I wanted to marry this man.

In the 24/7 Prayer Tower, Terry and I had visited, after the service in Jerusalem, a young woman had prayed to Jesus to provide me with a new husband. I was surprised. I'd never considered the eventuality of remarriage.

However, several months later, as, still filled with the balm of the Holy Spirit and the sight of couples, arm in arm, praising God together, I rode a suburban train home after Sunday worship at London's HTB Church; I heard a voice in my head say there was a man out there for me, a kind man. And he was waiting to meet me.

Clearly, I could do nothing with my feelings for Butch, right now. I was all packed to go home. I wouldn't know what to do, if I could.

I paused for a last, lingering look at myself on the rug. There I was, rope in hand, brow furrowed, hunting down my ibex.

Could I really hunt?

Perhaps, I thought, all my efforts to understand the rug's meaning had missed the issue.

Perhaps its purpose was to bring me here.

I found Terry downstairs in the kitchen, breakfasting on Cheerios. Running a finger along the counter, I felt about fourteen.

"By the way," I told her, "I like your brother."

Her eyebrows shot up. Her spoon wavered in mid-air. She worked at her mouthful. "Uh, when did this come up for you?"

"When he opened his front door."

She began to choke. I stepped forward to thump her on the back.

Initially, it turned out, I did have to pursue Butch with my lasso. He lacked self-confidence and was reluctant.

He came around.

We met in September. He proposed in February. We were married the following September — September 6, 2008.

I was very late for our wedding, nearly half an hour. The chauffeur wasn't from Fredericton. He took us to the wrong church. Neither myself, nor my U.K. family in the bridal car with me, knew how to redirect him.

As soon as we got to Smythe Street Cathedral, our pianist began to play and my bridesmaids processed quickly up the aisle. When I entered on my brother's arm, Butch almost ran to grab me and bring me up to join him on the podium.

I looked deep into his grey-green eyes and read the wave of emotion there as we stood, hands linked, to be married in the sight of God. Secure in our salvation and in one another, we spoke tender verses from Song of Songs:
This is my beloved and this is my friend.
Set me as a seal upon your heart, as a seal upon your arm, for love is as strong as death, jealousy as cruel as the grave.
My dove my perfect one is the only one.
My beloved is mine and I am his.
I am my beloved's and my beloved is mine

I felt rising inside of me the liquid love that God sends down through the Holy Spirit, in the same way I had experienced it, without realizing what it was, that first time in Jerusalem.

There, God took me, a despairing woman, who thought her happiness all behind her, and began a work of total transformation.

Bobbie Ann Cole
New Brunswick, Canada
www.shedoesnotfearthesnow.com
testimonytrain.com

> *"I heard a voice in my head say there was*
> *a man out there for me, a kind man.*
> *And he was waiting to meet me."*

René's Story

*"I made some wrong choices that ended
in more hurt and confusion."*

I had, in my youth, been engaged to a young man who found someone else while we were still together. Nursing that hurt for a long, long time I didn't date again for some time. Friends and family told me when you stop looking, that is when you will find someone. This didn't make much sense to me because I never got anything that I didn't work for. When I did date, I never fell in love.

At the age of 25 I decided to wait on the Lord because I had made some wrong choices that ended in more hurt and confusion. I did give up on love for a while, but then I decided that the Lord's timing is perfect and I would live my life. I wasn't waiting to begin my life anymore.

I got involved in church and charity work. I took up hobbies like playing guitar and singing in the church choir. I joined a cell group and built an amazing group of friends. I always longed for that deeper relationship with a soul mate, yet I never met anyone that I connected with at any of these activities. So I stopped looking altogether. At last I talked to God about it and I got a very real answer back: the time was not right, but to keep being faithful, and that God was proud of me for choosing to do it right. I felt in my heart that I would marry when I was a bit older, and that I would marry a man who had children already. I put it out of my mind but always held on to hope.

By the age of 32, I found myself single and without any prospects.

A few times I ventured into the weird world of online dating, but was sadly and sometimes comically disappointed by half-truths and full on lies. Some guys would profess to be believers so they knew they got a "good girl" on the line, but spending half an hour talking to them, you came to realize it wasn't true. So I pretty much gave up on that idea as well.

But one day following a Valentine's Day spent all by myself and dreading a future alone, I gave in to the typical single person thinking and joined yet another dating site. Within half an hour, a handful of guys had said, "Hello." One of them stood out. He asked if I would be available that Saturday, but he would like to meet me before the Saturday. I found this question strange but looking at his profile and the conversation we were having, I decided to give him a chance.

We went on our first date that Tuesday night and just hit it off. We talked all night, and he was so respectful and sweet. He was a joker and kept me laughing the whole time. I felt an immediate attraction, not only physically but also on a mental and emotional level. He was younger than I was, but had been married before which had matured him. He was also a dad of three.

The Saturday night turned out to be a Hillsong concert that he had two tickets to and wanted me to join him. From that point on we were inseparable. We loved spending time together and discovered we had many of the same interests and goals.

A while after we started dating he told me that he had only in recent years started following the Lord. He started going to church and had gone on a course to learn more about being a Christian. He was baptized at that course and right after getting out of the water asked the Lord to send him his wife. He had enough heartbreak and he was ready now for the Lord's perfect plan. The next day he went on the dating site and started speaking to only one woman – me. He said my smile attracted him first, but then he was intrigued when we talked. I asked about his kids and his life and he knew he just had to meet me.

A big test for our relationship was only a few months in. I had booked a holiday to Spain with a friend two months before I met my husband-to-be. It was paid up and there was no turning back. I had to go. It was a terrible thing for us both because we had been together such a short time and now we weren't going to be able to see each other or talk much for almost three weeks. We battled with this for a while. It turned out to be a horrible holiday, with me getting quite ill and my travel partner dictating our every move. I was never so glad to come back from a holiday as then. And at the airport, he was waiting for me with a coffee in hand and a smile on his face.

It wasn't long after that that we got engaged. His kids loved me, he loved me and I loved them. So we decided not to wait long. Eight months later at the age of 33, I was married for the first time. His little girl was our flower girl, and the twin boys were our ring bearers. We had a simple yet magical farm wedding, with lots of food and laughter and family. It was everything I dreamt of.

Getting married at 33 was a challenge in some ways. Not having been married before, I had no idea what to expect, even after all the stories and observations of other couples. Nothing can prepare you for marriage. Learning to adapt to another person's way of doing things, their world view and their anger triggers takes time. You bring your perceptions and opinions built up over years and you don't initially realize how much of an impact certain things have on you.

I've learnt a lot about myself and my husband over the past year of marriage. Chief on this list is that my happiness is integrally linked to his. If one of us is suffering, so is the other. I also learnt that priorities change when you are married, and that some things are important to discuss while other things are best left unsaid. I think a marriage relationship is hard but worth it. If you walk the road with the Lord, He does help and work with you on your marriage. And without love it will never last. The best feeling in the world is every morning when my husband and I pray together for our marriage and our family and our lives. It feels like this was what I had been waiting for my whole life. And God knew who I needed.

After all the heartbreak and the waiting, and the bad advice from well-meaning third parties, the wait was worth it. In my entire life I had never been so close to anyone, male or female. I had never found someone who knew me so well or understood me so well. From the start we were in sync, one of those couples who finish each other's sentences. It was worth waiting for. It was worth skipping all the cheap thrills and meaningless dates. It was worth keeping pure for all those years, and focusing my energy on God. It was worth making the most of the single years, pursuing hobbies and travels while I had no family commitments.

I never expected to meet the man of my dreams on a website. I never expected it all to go so quickly and end so well. At the time of this writing, we are expecting a baby now. I don't know if I am ready for motherhood either, although having three little ones that visit every second week and school holidays has prepared me somewhat. But just like with marriage, I am leaving this in God's hands. He knows what I can handle and His timing has been perfect all through my life. I get the feeling He knows what he is doing.

René du Preez
Johannesburg, South Africa

*"After all the heartbreak and the waiting,
and the bad advice from well-meaning
third parties, the wait was worth it."*

Cathey's Story

*"It felt like so long since I had been in love,
I was heart-sick, doubting my own character
and attractiveness, wondering if I was
ever going to meet someone."*

I can't remember when I first met my future husband, but I started to get to know him at the end of 2005. I was 32 when we started dating. We married in 2010, four and a half years later.

Although we had been dating for a while, his proposal was a complete surprise - both seemingly contradicting and fulfilling prophecies that I had held close to my heart for many years in a most incredible way.

I had been part of the same church family for around 15 years; I became a Christian there, was baptised there, joined the youth group, ran a kids' work, and was part of the loving extended family that our church was (and still is) so very gifted in. I had a boyfriend for a couple of years until I was 20, then nothing serious for 12 years. During that time I was given many kind "prophecies" about marriage (some with dates attached!) and I slowly learned that unless the prophecy came with undeniable confirmation, I should accept the loving gesture it was given with, but not the word.

Around 2003 I visited Toronto Christian Fellowship for a Catch The Fire conference. I hadn't planned on going, but some friends dropped out of a trip and I was able to take their place. It was a trip covered in favour. Both myself and a friend travelling together were upgraded to business class, drank champagne and were able to sleep in a bed on the long flight to and from the UK. Another friend miraculously received a golden filling in their tooth, others who were on the verge of setting aside their relationship with God found themselves swept off their feet and romanced by Him.

And I was given a word that completely turned my world upside down.

It felt like so long since I had been in love, I was heart-sick, doubting my own character and attractiveness, wondering if I was ever going to meet someone. My church family were telling me that "it will just happen one day," but I was becoming more and more aware that they didn't actually know this for a fact. At the same time I was trusting that one day, God would find the right man for me; I had prayed for him and understood that for whatever reason, wherever he was, if I hadn't met him yet, either one or both of us wasn't ready for that to happen. I just wanted it to happen sooner rather than later!

On the first night of the Catch the Fire conference, I was worshipping and felt as if God was asking me, "W*hat if the plans I have for you are better than the plans that you have for you?*" from which I understood He was giving me a choice; I could have marriage, kids, family and everything, or I could trust Him with the plans He had.

I was stunned. Not get married? Not have children? I didn't want to be alone; I didn't want to learn how to knit to fill endless hours of solitude! No. No no no no no. I struggled with worship, I hardly heard any of the conference. Every hour of that conference was filled with the question, "What if . . ."

On the last night of the conference all of the delegates had the opportunity to line up to receive prayer. I joined them, still with this unanswered question. The ministry team came along the line, praying, ministering – and completely bypassed me. I was left standing whilst people all around were shaking, crying, lying on the floor, laughing.

It was then I decided that if God had a plan for me then that was better than the perfect imaginary world I had created and that was where I wanted to be. I wanted to be in God's plan, not my plan. At that moment I put all of my hopes of marriage and family aside in exchange for a greater hope. God would look after me in my old age and it was going to be more exciting than I could imagine.

Within seconds of accepting God's plan for my life, the ministry team turned up in front of me - completely unbidden - and began to pray and prophesy over me. The single verse that they gave me was the word that confirmed everything that I had been praying and at the same time was the promise of God's favour.

"Delight yourself also in the Lord, and He shall give you the desires of your heart." (Psalm 37:4 NKJV)

Now that I had given everything over to Jesus, He was the centre of my heart's desire. But at the same time He seemed to be saying that my desire for love and family might still be part of His plan, although given the decision I had just made, I certainly wasn't going to expect it!

I stopped praying for a husband and started praying for God's plan. Well, most of the time. I stopped waiting for Mr Right to turn up and got on with doing exciting things on my own. I started travelling, visiting Italy and Turkey among other places and I started to learn how to Salsa!

When people prayed for me for a husband I thanked them and happily told them that God had given me a specific word to say that marriage wasn't part of His plan for me, that He had even better things in store.

I went on quite a few dates over the next couple of years. I believe there's something inherently attractive about a girl who isn't afraid to be single and who is living life to the full. I enjoyed dating and learned a lot about what I did and didn't like in a guy and in relationships.

I started to spend quite a bit of time with a chap from church. He knew how to Salsa and took me out dancing on a Friday night. We started dating and were both under no illusions that this was going anywhere. Me: because of the word from God, him: because he had a failed marriage and two grown up sons. After a few months people at church started asking if we were serious and within a year I was getting hints about hats and wedding bells. I was able to say, quite honestly, that not only was that not our plan, but God's plan too. Eventually we were left to our rather quirky relationship, which suited us both.

One dear friend heard my testimony and decided that she was still going to pray for a good man for me. I have to say that I still hoped.

This chap and I became close friends. He was a new Christian and we enjoyed some interesting discussions as his faith grew. We enjoyed dancing together, especially in worship. We would often take walks in the park together. I fell utterly in love with him, and, although sad that marriage would never figure, I was still holding onto

God's promise that His plan is perfect and was even better than I could imagine for myself. That promise is what kept me with this guy, when a logical person might decide to go looking elsewhere for someone prepared to make a commitment.

In August 2009 I found myself following a treasure hunt set especially for me in a beautiful local park. It was a beautiful day, as the words, "Would you marry me," materialised from the clues. I was stunned. I discovered later that a conversation with his housemate had lead him to believe that there was still hope for real love. (His housemate was very close friends with the woman who continued to pray for me.)

When I said, "Yes," strawberries and champagne were taken from his bag and we enjoyed a romantic picnic in a Japanese style garden.

We then spent a week without telling anyone, except our church leaders, what we had decided. There were a lot of now crucial conversations that we had never had because we never intended to plan a future together. That week allowed us to unpack our hopes and our dreams, ask questions and know that if we wanted to, we could change our minds without any drama.

It was a memorable moment when we stood in front of our church family and told them we were engaged. We were received with a standing ovation.

Our wedding day was the happiest day of my life to that point, but I have to say that since then I have been constantly blown away by the goodness of our God. I have been happier than I ever believed possible and am enjoying being right in the middle of where I believe God wants me to be. Our wedding day was just the start.

Looking back I see God's promise for my future completely fulfilled. He never said, "No," to marriage, He just allowed me to trust Him first and foremost. The fact that I was prepared to give up those dreams allowed the man of my dreams time to heal and to hear from God himself without any pressure or expectations from me.

I am so thankful for every day with my husband: more so because I waited so long for him, I think. After being single so long I was terrified that we would both be set in our ways and that living together would be horrific. This wasn't the case at all. I am daily so grateful for all of the little things he does, for every word he encourages me with and every opportunity I have to encourage him.

Advice to those still waiting and hoping: remember that we are not the only part of the equation. God is working in us and in our future partner and learning patience is just a tiny part of all the things He is bringing together for us. We need to be ourselves, not projecting what we think is a more attractive version of ourselves. Let's face it, that kind of façade is exhausting! Let's do what interests *us*, not what we think men might find attractive.

Finally: if you have a prophecy that you know without doubt comes from God then THAT is the one to put on your wall, your mirror, your desk, in your purse. Hold fast to Him and enjoy the ride.

Cathey Hawes
Auckland, New Zealand
(by way of Manchester, United Kingdom)

*"I decided that if God had a plan
for me then that was better than the
perfect imaginary world I had created
and that was where I wanted to be."*

Gillian's Story

"I had many well-meaning marrieds that would
ask me, particularly at weddings, 'You are such
a lovely young lady, when is it going
to be your turn?'"

My life plan was to marry young (in my early 20s), spend a number of years building my marriage and getting to know my husband, then have 3 or 4 children by the time I was 30. Did God have a different plan for me!!

I had two serious relationships, one in high school, the other in university and then the long drought began. With my last relationship ending when I was 20, by the time I got to 28, I was starting to wonder if it was ever going to happen. I was trying to be positive; I didn't want to be desperate "looking for love in all the wrong places" and putting guys off. As each year rolled by, I set my heart on God and serving the church and decided, "I'll leave this up to you, Lord."

Well, eight years is long time! During that time I never met anyone I was remotely interested in. Thinking maybe I was too fussy, and being told I was by well-meaning others, I went through a season where I said to myself, "Okay, if someone asks you out on a date you are going to say, 'Yes,' no matter what your first impression is." So I dated 4 guys, 2 of which were non-Christian, one of which was a blind date, all resulting in the awkward, "I am sorry I just don't see this going anywhere," conversation a few weeks into it.

I couldn't blame myself for not trying, and I often argued with God about 1 Corinthians 7:38, where Paul says it is better to be single, and wondering if that was what He had called me to, but reminding Him that without marriage we couldn't go forth and multiply! What is happening, Lord? I also had many well-meaning marrieds that would ask me, particularly at weddings, "You are such a lovely young lady, when is it going to be your turn?" To which I would respond appropriately, while in my head screaming, "DON'T YOU THINK I ASK GOD THAT ALL THE TIME?!?"

In 2008 I met Andrew after he responded to our flatmate wanted ad on the local Christian accommodation website. We needed a flatmate, he needed a room and a place to park his boat; it was perfect! As with any new guy that appears in your life during your late 20's everyone started asking if maybe he was the one. Of course he wasn't! He was way too young (2½ years younger to be exact).

So our friendship began and what a great friendship it was. We loved hanging out together, he challenged me in my walk with God and I started to realise – I think he is interested in me. I did everything to ensure it was clear that we were only friends.

At the beginning of 2009, right before I turned 28, I had a discussion with God and told Him, "This is going to be, 'The Year of the Husband!'" And so the prayer and fasting began. I prayed once a month for my husband. In the meantime Andrew had cottoned on to the fact that I wasn't interested and sent me an email in the April of that year to tell me that he had indeed been interested in me, but just wanted to let me know that he wasn't anymore and hoped that it didn't affect our friendship. Relief flooded through me, no awkward conversation was to be had and we could remain great friends.

The prayer and fasting continued; this WAS The Year of the Husband! During this time a few eligible guys came into my life and early in the year I was feeling optimistic and full of faith. But as the year marched on, I began to wonder, "Is this really going to happen?" And my faith began to dwindle. Also playing at the back of my mind was Andrew's email. Did I like him more than a friend? I started to feel irritated that he hadn't given me the opportunity to say, "No," to him and had just decided for me.

In October 2009, our flat chose to do a Daniel fast with The Year of the Husband at the top of my list. A few days into it, Andrew emailed me to ask: 1. Was I going to eat my potatoes hot or cold, and 2. Were we strictly friends/flatmates? This freaked me out, so I took a while to respond with: 1. Hot, and 2. I wasn't sure. This was the start of our relationship.

We got married in January 2011, 2 months before my 30th birthday. So much for my plan, but I know that this was all a part of God's plan for me, that I needed 10 months of fasting for God to change my heart and show me what He had put right in front of me. Now almost 3 years into our marriage, I can only confirm if you put your trust in Him and open your life to Him, He really does have the best for you.

The main obstacles in our relationship early on were church related. We were both very passionate about the local church we each belonged to and the process of God changing my heart and releasing me into this new season of my life was painful. Had I not spent a lot of time praying about it and talking to Andrew, I might have given Andrew up, thinking that the church I went to was more important. But God has taught me that while it is important to be fully committed to the church, we also need to remind ourselves we are committed to Him first.

I think there are pros and cons to everything. Although I wish I had met and married Andrew earlier in my life so I could have shared more with him, I know that I am blessed to have had the time to discover who I am and do things for me. I feel I am a better wife and, as I know who I am in Christ, I was able to go into our marriage a whole, confident person.

For the person reading this who is still waiting, like I was, wondering if God has called you to a life of singleness like Paul, don't lose hope! Place your trust in Him, keep your heart and mind open and give people a chance. See this time as an opportunity to keep discovering who God has made you and work on who you would want to be as a wife so you are well prepared for when your husband does come along!

After being married I am fully convinced I would rather be single than married to the wrong person. Don't ever fall into the trap that anyone is better than no-one. If possible, marry someone who is or will be your best friend! You spend way more time just doing life than all the romantic stuff. The rest of your life is a long time to be married to someone you were once attracted to, but now don't even like!

Gillian Ardern
Auckland, New Zealand

> *"As each year rolled by, I set my heart on God*
> *and serving the church and decided,*
> *'I'll leave this up to you, Lord.'"*

Jill's Story

*"I never yearned for a boyfriend
or a husband like so many others did."*

At 21, I was working in retail and was one of the worship leaders at the local church my family attended in Sheffield, in the UK. This was an exciting time of church growth and expansion and it was then that I met an evangelist called, Terry Eckersley. He would've been 31 at the time.

I remember being introduced at the end of a church service. Someone said, "Let me introduce you to Terry; he's got an amazing testimony." I thought, "He's a bit full on!!!! Waving his hands and waxing lyrical about how Jesus had changed his life." But Terry thought that this was everyone's experience and that Jesus was worth getting excited about and sharing this with everyone he met!

Throughout the years, Terry became very good friends with my mum, Janet. As he hadn't had the privilege of being brought up within a caring, loving, Christian home, she also became a surrogate mum for him, as well. During all that time there was no connection between Terry and myself. He would occasionally be invited for Sunday lunch where he would turn up, eat lunch, then fall asleep on the sofa! (Cheek!!)

If anyone had said to me then that I would some day be married to Terry those many years ago, I probably would have laughed in disbelief.

I continued my work within retail and worship leading at my church and within church plants. Contented with my life of work, church, family and my wonderful season of singleness, I never yearned for a boyfriend or a husband like so many others did. I also would say I never felt right about just "dating" people in church. This may be different for other people, but I didn't believe it was right for me. I wanted to be a good example for others watching my life. And I never liked the idea of potentially dating someone else's future husband.

I found myself in my early 30's serving on worship team in a church plant in Leeds when my family and I were invited to a dinner party at one of the leaders' homes. The conversation began to come up around dating and future partners when Eddie (one of the leaders) said, "Judy and I have recommended that people write a list of 'ten things' they are looking for in a future partner. Everyone we have encouraged to do this has met their partners within 6 months." Wow! That seemed very specific and very quick! But I also thought it was interesting and maybe I should give it a go.

Now the list I wrote didn't contain complicated things and everyone's will be different, but if you were to make a list, I would ask you, what are the most important, lasting things you would be looking for? Mine contained things that were important to me. And it really helped me focus rather than be general.

Meanwhile, Terry always kept in touch with Mum and was invited every year on Boxing Day for a second Christmas. Not much had changed. He ate, talked and slept on the sofa. But God was prospering him, and his effectiveness in many areas was growing.

It wasn't until my mum became very ill in December 2005 that things began to slowly shift in our friendship. There had been so many changes in my life, but one of the biggest and best was the change in my relationship with Terry. Instead of my mum and Terry talking, it was Terry and *me* talking. It was amazing that I had known Terry for over ten years, but now I was starting to see him in a different light. We were getting on really well. We would chat regularly on the phone and he would come up north to see me (not just the family). We'd go out for meals and we were just getting closer.

Terry was now the CEO of the YMCA in Woking, and as I became very impressed with the work he was doing, I wanted to serve there. Incidentally, a perfect opportunity had come up to do music workshops with disadvantaged youth.

Terry placed an advert with the local Woking churches for accommodation for me as a "volunteer young woman at the Woking YMCA," and we'd been relying on this advert to get me a place to stay. Time was running out and just as Terry was typing an email to another YMCA that provided housing in the hope of getting me somewhere to stay, a phone call came from a local Christian couple who had a room for me at no charge. Truly a miracle! This couple had a large, detached mansion with three spare rooms and they became good friends to Terry and myself.

As I served on team at Woking YMCA, we started to fall in love. I had seen another side to Terry when he dropped everything to visit my sick mother. This was a tremendous time for both of us, but equally challenging. We had known each other so long that we were like brother and sister, but now it was all changing and we didn't want to get it wrong or hurt each other. Terry and I were both praying about this and I subsequently was to find out that God was giving Terry a green light.

Our first official date was when Terry was invited to Buckingham Palace in recognition of the work he had done in the community. He was able to have someone accompany him and my mum hinted heavily that he should take me. So Terry asked if I would like to come and I said, "Yes!" (Who wouldn't!?) We went through the formalities of security and being commanded by the Lord Lieutenant to attend the Queen's Garden Party at Buckingham Palace.

One day, after a sort of work review over lunch in London one Saturday, Terry proposed to me. I was so surprised, I was laughing in shock! Terry said, "You'd better make your mind up; we're booked into Tiffany's just around the corner." I got to pick out my engagement ring from my favourite jewellers. He then took me to Paris, first class, on the EuroStar and we ended up under the Eiffel Tower by moonlight!

In less than nine months, we were married in a beautiful Old Village Church in Woking. I had sung at so many weddings that were almost a contemporary Christian conveyer belt, that we both wanted to be married the traditional way. We had a beautiful dream, sun-filled, love- and faith-filled service. I was marrying the man of my dreams and my best friend! After the service we went to a local hotel for the wedding breakfast. Everyone who came was intrinsically a part of our journey, an encouragement and support to all we had become.

And remember my list? I had forgotten about the list until I found it one day after we married. From writing the list to being engaged to Terry was about 10 months. And we married 6 months after that. God really does give us the desires of our heart as we delight ourselves in Him. I think Derek Prince has written a good book on this called, "God is a Matchmaker."

Over time, we all change. And preconceived ideas we have of others can be challenged. I remember forming my "idea" of what Terry was like. But the person I got to know, fell in love with and married, was a totally different person to that.

What at first didn't seem like a fit at all, became a perfect fit in God. We have, at the time of this writing, been blissfully married for nearly seven years. This has remained through the heights, depths and all the challenges that life can bring as we keep Christ the centre of our lives and marriage.

I do believe there is the right person out there for everyone. As Terry would say, their "perfect fit."

Jill Eckersley
United Kingdom
www.terryeckersley.co.uk

> *"What at first didn't seem like a fit at all,*
> *became a perfect fit in God."*

Nella's Story

*"I fell in love a few times, but was too shy
and too timid to show my feelings, too
scared of making a fool of myself."*

Ronnie and I met when I was 13 and he was 18 years old. He was best man and my sister was bridesmaid at his brother's and my cousin's marriage. My mother thought that he was a very nice young man and I said "No, he combs his hair backwards!" After the wedding our paths separated for the next 28 years . . .

I was a very shy child and later a shy adult and though I had various lovely friends, I never really had a boyfriend. I often told Jesus about my wishes to also have that someone special. We were a lovely group of youngsters at church and apart from attending church, we also did quite a lot of things together, like youth camps, etc.

Later on all my cousins and friends were married and had children and though I was still single, was mostly included in get togethers and outings. All this while I kept on talking to Jesus about my singleness. I fell in love a few times, but was too shy and too timid to show my feelings, too scared of making a fool of myself.

When I was about 28 years old a new guy came to work at my office. We became friends and later became engaged. This did not work out, but I can only thank God in all earnest because he was not a child of God and we would surely have gotten divorced at some time.

All this time, through the years, Ronnie and his parents, who lived very far from us on a farm, came visiting our city on holiday and always came to see my family. (I cannot remember this, but Ronnie told me eventually that on one such a visit I did not even come out of my room to see them!)

Following my mother's death in 1979, my father remarried. And after my broken engagement, I decided to move to Cape Town where I got involved in church and the youth meetings there. I was quite involved with the lovely friends I met and while I was happy, I still lacked that special person in my life.

Friends kept introducing me to single men, but I just never felt that special feeling towards any of them. During all this time I kept talking to Jesus about this and I kept on praying for my future husband. I asked God to bless him in abundance even though I had no assurance that I would ever get married and had no idea who my husband would be!

I have a friend who got married reasonably late in life and had a daughter, but her husband could not provide well enough for them. They truly struggled financially and that made quite a negative impression on me. While I asked God again for that special person in my life, I knew I would rather remain single and happy than married, perhaps with a child, and struggling. I asked Him to please give me somebody I can admire and whose capabilities were such that I would be proud of him. I also asked that this future husband of mine and I be best friends, and that he be willing that we as a couple read the Bible and pray together every evening at bedtime, and in the mornings at the start of each day.

All my life I adored children and dogs. Having a dog or two helped a lot during my solitude and in my longing to have a child. I always wanted a son as my parents only had two daughters. One evening, after talking to God about this longing, I read an article in a magazine about an older first time mother. Again I brought this to my Heavenly Father. I often asked Him for a son - if possible an intelligent and healthy one and also (if possible) one with blue eyes.

That evening after reading the article again and talking to God about it all, I opened my Bible and my eyes fell onto Psalm 113. Then I came to verse 9: "He settles the barren women in her home as a happy mother of children." (WEB). The feeling about this verse was so strong, I felt this was His promise to me and I wrote the date next to the verse. As I thought about that promise as the months and years went by, and as I was getting older without finding a husband, I thought that maybe God would give me a widower as a husband and that I will thus be a mother for his children.

When I was about to turn 40, a lady friend and I went on holiday to visit my sister at Klerksdorp, a far away town from Cape Town, then to visit my cousin and her husband on the farm near Mafikeng in the North West Province of South Africa. While we were visiting on the farm, Ronnie, who farmed nearby, came round to greet us. I suddenly knew that I respected this man, but that was it. At my sister's place I got teased by them about Ronnie and I still told them to stop it as I respected him too much to have fun being made of him.

Shortly after I was back home in Cape Town, I wrote letters to everyone to thank them for their kindness during our visit. It was then that Ronnie and I started corresponding with one another. He then started to phone me at times, then came the 1200 kilometres to visit me, and eventually we started a relationship.

It was during one of these visits to Cape Town that he asked me to marry him the last evening before he had to return to the farm. My answer was that I first wanted to pray. I remember talking to Jesus about it just after he left when suddenly I just got that knowing certainty in my heart. That was before the advent of cell phones, so I sent him a telegram with my reply, and then wrote him a long letter telling him about it. He told me later that he collected the letter from his post office box, but did not open it at once because his mother was with him in the vehicle, and that he was so excited that he went past the turn off to the farm and had to turn back.

Ronnie came visiting me again towards the end of November 1993 and we went to buy my dream engagement ring. Then we drove to Bloubergstrand beach, where we took a long walk on the beach and back to my old car, where we got engaged! It was just the two of us and it was even more special as I love the sight of Table Mountain and the sea which was clearly visible in front of us.

Our wedding was on 2 April 1994 in the church in Vryburg, Ronnie's home town and we had a lovely luncheon with our family and some friends afterwards. I thought then that we were too old, to have children (me being 41 and Ronnie 46) but Ronnie so much wanted one that I agreed to see whether I would become pregnant before the end of November that year. But during May I became aware that I was pregnant and - listen nicely - our blue eyed, completely healthy baby boy was born on 5 March 1995 - two weeks early and eleven months after our wedding day. That was seven years after God's promise to me in Psalm 113:9 as noted in my Bible.

Although we were older and it was a first marriage for both of us, we did not have any real adjustments between the two of us. We were then, and still are, best friends. We never go to sleep or begin our day before reading and praying together and we talk about everything. And I am absolutely proud of his abilities in everything. He is a successful farmer as well as an income tax consultant and has a helping spirit. God is so, so good to me!

I would encourage other single ladies to be on constant speaking terms with our Lord Jesus. Tell Him about all your heart's desires and trust Him. He loves you and knows you better than anybody does.

Make the part of Matthew 6 verse 32 ". . . and your Heavenly Father knows . . ." part of your every breath. After Ronnie came all the way to ask me to marry him, Mary's song in Luke 1 from verse 46 onwards, filled my whole being.

Our God lives and He loves YOU as well as me!

Nella Crafford
Stella, South Africa

> *"During all this time I kept talking to Jesus and I kept on praying for my future husband."*

Karen's Story

*"I thought for sure that God would bring
me my husband while I was serving Him
in full-time ministry, but He didn't."*

I am the daughter, granddaughter, niece and cousin of pastors. In fact, I guess you could say that the ministry is our family business. I grew up in a great family; I never even had the desire to rebel against my folks because of my respect for them and their ministry. So it wasn't a stretch to find myself deciding to move to California to attend the same Bible College all those in ministry in my family attended (12 relatives in all!), affectionately dubbed LIFE Bridal College by the many students who met their mates there.

I discovered that my mom had my grandfather's high school class ring and thought it was pretty cool looking, so my mom gave it to me. It was pretty small for a men's ring because my grandfather had it sized to my grandmother's finger. I decided to wear it as a reminder to wait for my husband, much like the purity rings that became popular years later.

Although I had my share of dates while in college, I never felt like I had met the man God was preparing for me, whom I affectionately called, "my man after God's own heart." I refused to date non-Christians, so aside from college and church, my scope of possibilities was limited. Don't get me wrong, not everyone who attended the college got married; in fact, some of the professors were single. I thought choosing to avoid spending any time with them would keep me from getting the same . . . affliction – singlehood. Little did I know that I was in store for a good long lesson in patience.

There was a guy in college that I was interested in, but unfortunately every time we attempted a relationship, God revealed to me a character issue and sent up one of those freeway-sized red flags in my heart stopping me from getting further involved. I remember one evening when he was passing back through town a few years after we had been in school together and I heard what seemed like an audible voice from God saying, "Noooo! Do you want to be the spiritual head of your home? If you pursue a relationship with him, you will be." There is nothing more that I want in my life than to be in His perfect will, so I listened. A few years later, I heard he had married and when I contacted him to say congratulations, he said he felt pushed into the marriage and wished that he had pursued me. I was so grateful that God cared enough for me years earlier to have given me that check in my spirit.

I recall on many occasions, friends, especially at church, would come up to me and say, "I just don't get it. I don't understand why you are still single." I knew they meant it as a compliment, so I always took it that way . . . but when someone unknowingly tells you they were trying to figure out what was wrong with you to be afflicted with singleness, well, it smarts, even when you know they are trying to pay you a compliment. What's more, Satan, on occasion, would use that as a tool to try to discourage me.

I had the opportunity to work with an incredibly godly man who attended Bible College with my parents, aunts and uncles. He was the Bible College president and was divorced, but had been single for a very long time. One day at the office, he showed me a gorgeous emerald ring he had bought while he was a missionary years earlier in Panama. He said God had promised him that some day he would get married again, so he bought that ring as a reminder of the promise.

He said that on occasion when he was feeling down, he would pull the ring from his desk drawer and remind himself of God's promise, and he'd be fine again. Although I wore my grandfather's ring every day, on occasion I would stop and think the same thing. How like God is that, that He would bring this example to me as if to say, "See, you aren't the only one!" I consider it one of the greatest blessings to have been a part of his life when he met his Promise. And what a testimony of God's faithfulness to our students . . . and to me! I remember the day he told me about her as if it had happened yesterday and I told him that it gave me hope that God would answer my promise too.

I thought for sure that God would bring me my husband while I was serving Him in full-time ministry, but He didn't. Hey, I was serving Him, right? Wouldn't that be a great story to share? But it didn't happen that way. It wasn't until a few years after I moved back home to New Mexico. I hadn't dated in several years and there were no prospects. I had come to terms with my singleness and for most of the time, was content.

In fact, while on staff at the Bible College, I was blessed with the opportunity to mentor several young ladies whom I would always tell, I'd rather be single and happy than married and miserable! The College President's story taught me it was OK to get down once in a while, but don't wallow in it!

In 2008 when the economy took the major dive, I lost my job and was out of work for several months. As a result, I took the first job that I was offered making half what I had made before. All I knew is that I had to get back to work before I lost my mind! I was so miserable in that job that I accepted a new job working for a company I probably never would have considered before.

I remember listening to a Christian radio station on my way in to work on my first day and as I drove up, the Matt Maher song "Hold Us Together," came on the radio. The line "This is the first day of the rest of your life," rang out in my heart. Silly me, I thought it was God's direction about my salary! But deep in my heart, I had hoped that He would bring an answer to my own special promise, that I would indeed be married some day.

Over a year later when I was 43, Michael started at our company as a temp on a special project. He worked the next hall over from me and his boss' office was at the end of my hallway. Our office had great camaraderie, so we all laughed and joked and yelled down the hall at each other. I remember saying to my coworker (who was a self-described recovering Catholic and had no relationship with God), "I think Michael might be interested in me." To which she replied, "Uhh, you think?" I explained to her that I couldn't date him if he wasn't a Christian.

I later had a similar conversation with my boss who was also a Christian and within a couple of days, Michael happened to be chatting with her in her office. The walls had large floor to ceiling panels with cracks in them so big I could see her, so it was easy to overhear the conversation even when you weren't trying. They started talking about when he and his son went on a missions trip to Mexico with Youth With A Mission (YWAM). As soon as he left her office and literally as he walked three steps passed mine, she called me and said, "Did you hear that?!" She knew the standard I lived by and was almost giddy with excitement.

About two days later, Michael stopped by my office and asked if I knew a good small church in the area. I invited him to my church and he showed up that Sunday. If you have sisters like mine, I'm sure you can imagine the laser focus on him when he sat down next to me. I'm surprised we didn't have smoke rising from our heads from burn holes caused by their laser-like attention! My sister asked me who he was and I told her he was a friend from work, to which she quickly insisted on telling me to invite him over for our Sunday family dinner. I expected him to decline, but he surprised me and accepted. He then spent the next two hours trying to eat as he was peppered with questions from the family. Talk about running the gauntlet on day one!

After lunch, we stood outside my sister's house chatting for over an hour and ended by planning our first real date later that week. I still count that Sunday as our first date and wrote about it that night in my journal. As our relationship quickly progressed, I read back about that day and discovered that Sunday was 10/10/2010. Seven months later and a week before he headed back for one final trip to Iraq as a civilian contractor with the military, he proposed and I accepted.

Six months later, we were married on 11/11/2011. As my dad gave me away, I quietly slipped my grandfather's ring to him, and stepped into the fulfillment of God's promise. It was an honor to have my dad, my uncle, who, for many years was my pastor, and the college president officiate at our wedding. What a day of celebration!

Now I am reminded of God's faithfulness whenever the calendar changes to November 11th or when I happen to look at the clock and it is 11:11.

If you find yourself single and past your twenties, be encouraged! God has a plan for you! Wait on the Lord and renew your strength in Him because He's preparing a blessing for you beyond what you can imagine.

If you are a younger lady, hold out for God's best! If I can do it, you can do it! Set a standard of excellence in your relationships. Listen to His still quiet voice guide and direct you. Wait . . . and be prepared to have your socks blessed off. I did and I'm now sockless.

Karen Hyde Hobbs
Albuquerque, New Mexico, USA

> *"Deep in my heart, I had hope that He*
> *would bring an answer to my own special*
> *promise, that I would indeed be married*
> *some day."*

Jude's Story

*"The hardest for me was not having children
and the 30's, with its loud clock, was painful."*

My single life had moments of great joy and great pain. I had wonderful friends and family who fortunately never put pressure on me to "find" a man (as if I wasn't looking). Fulfilling work has always been the answer for me (and still is) to live a satisfied life.

I got stuck for many years "waiting" for God to bring a husband along and fell into the "God's will" way of thinking when one did not materialise. I also, in hindsight, allowed cultural and "Christian" expectations to filter out most available men (although there weren't a huge number to filter out to start with!). By cultural I mean voices such as, "Don't marry outside your social class," "Make sure they have a tertiary qualification," etc.

The Christian voices were more along the lines of toxic religion such as, "There is only one right person for you," "Don't marry a divorced person," etc. When married people say, "I just knew it was right," they are saying so with the privilege and benefit of hindsight. Perhaps a more healthy way to approach finding a partner is not looking for the one "right" person, but looking for someone who could become right for you through communication and negotiation.

The hardest for me was not having children and the 30's, with its loud clock, was painful. But again, if I had had a more meaningful career in my early 30's, this would not have been so painful.

I decided half way through my 30's that you don't have to be a biological parent to parent children. I had become involved in running a youth group from my early 30's and then I retrained as a high school teacher. Those mentoring roles were valuable to me and those I mentored.

Giving up hope, which I did from time to time, was indeed hope-less and brought no life. So I decided to hope in God's goodness and know whatever happened, it would all be OK in the end. Cultivating and having close women friends is probably the best thing you can do in life and I would encourage any single women to do so as you still need and love them as much after marriage!!

The most unhelpful things I endured being single:

I decided after living for 20 years in one city to take a risk and move to a new city where a group of friends were living. I thought the Lord might give me the promise of a job or a partner or preferably both. But in His wisdom he let me make a good measured decision to make up my own mind and go. After a month in the new city, I met my husband to be! We met at church and I was attracted to him by the way he treated people and his lack of victimhood, even though he had been through a very rough season. He was, and is, always positive about his outlook.

So I met my husband when I was 42 and married at 44! For me, the option of having children, I decided, was passed. I did not want to be 50 taking little Johnnie or Susie to school! My decision was affirmed when my then man stated very firmly he did not want children!

Being set in your ways is always a choice. I expect that if you have left home and lived by yourself, you are certainly more likely to choose to be set in your ways. For most of my life, I chose to live with others. Living with others always tempers your own behaviour, allowing you to become very tolerant of others' habits. So for me, living with my husband when we married was not such a big deal. There were naturally negotiations about partnering with housework, etc., as I was not about to pick up that one myself. Advice – negotiate that at the start!!

The experience of waiting has given me perspective that many people don't have. Getting married later is likely to make you more appreciative of your mate. It taught me that life doesn't turn out how you planned, but that experience can be used for so much good. And the waiting taught me to hold onto God in a way that I haven't since I have been married, and if I'm honest, I was closer to Him and spent more time with Him before I was married.

I would encourage a single girlfriend who is still waiting for her husband-to-be:

* To be proactive about looking for him. While I never had the courage to go online for a partner (and that was in its infancy when I was in my 30's), I think it is a very valid way of meeting someone if done carefully.
* That she's not about to mess with the will of God if she starts actively looking.
* To coach herself through rejection. Just because a guy doesn't want to go out with her, she (the entirety of who she is) is not rejected. And take risks!

Jude Van Wichen Miller
Auckland, New Zealand

> *"I decided to hope in God's goodness*
> *and know whatever happened,*
> *it would all be OK in the end."*

Lorinda's Story

*"There were times of real sadness,
desperation, and yes, fear, at the thought
of being alone for the rest of my life."*

Ah, the season of Christian singleness!

I grew up in a church culture where people married young
– 18-20 years – so if you weren't married by 21, or at
least with a prospect in sight, there was something wrong
with you. Add to that divorced parents and a wobbly faith
and you were essentially done for.

Despite walking away from my roots for a time, as some
of us are wont to do, my journey through 'The Single
Season' as a Christian felt a little like being snowed in, in
a mountain cabin with supplies running low during a long,
arduous winter – no end in sight and fast running out of
patience. As if wrestling with God over the issue of
whom, what, when and where were not enough, many
lovely and well-meaning Christian people I knew felt it
their duty to "console" me with "encouraging" phrases
such as:

"Perhaps this is God's way of helping you to work things
out in your own life."

"You're a very strong, independent woman. It'll take
someone really special to keep up with you!"

"Just focus on Jesus and He'll bring the right person along
at the right time."

Yes, I can hear the collective groan; see the rolling of eyes and heads shaking in disbelief as we speak!

Despite some of this well-meaning "encouragement" coming from older Christian couples I knew and respected, some of it came from what I called "The Smug-Marrieds Club" – I'm sure you know the type: 21 year old, newly-married couples who have known each other 5 minutes before embarking on a lifetime of confetti-covered forever love. My cynical nature had the upper hand back then, and while I have no doubt there was a genuine desire to be encouraging, it's hard to receive that kind of encouragement from someone whose experience of waiting for Mr Right has covered the three years after high school – compared with 10 years of longing, an aging body and a ticking clock.

There were times where God was able to show me the joy of real contentment in being single– including a period of time where I lived overseas and relished the freedom of being able to do whatever, whenever, wherever with any one or more of my friends at the drop of a hat. There were also times of real sadness, desperation and yes, fear, at the thought of being alone for the rest of my life.

It wasn't just the thought of missing out on companionship, but also the weight of having to provide for myself for the rest of my life along with the prospect of never being a mum – something I had always wanted to be. I struggled incredibly in those times – wrestling with God and myself. You see, once upon a time I had been in a relationship – a worldly one mind you – but nevertheless one that had afforded me a view, albeit a distorted one, of what being married might be like. And it was something I longed to taste again – only this time,

God's way. I'd made a bit of a hash of doing things my way so I thought I'd let Him take the reins on this one.

Early in 2004, on my return from Italy and in preparing to return there for work, I was introduced to the man who would become my husband. It was a casual meeting from my end, as my focus was on returning to Italy. I had absolutely no desire to meet anyone, and I had no intention of deviating from my plan. God, however, not only has a sense of humour but also His own agenda. His ways are definitely not our ways – and that is probably a good thing!

One morning as I waited on the platform for my morning train to work, I was taken by surprise as I prayed silently to myself. My prayer was simply a request to know who this man was supposed to be to me. The answer: Your husband. I can tell you that this was not the response I was expecting. This was the first time I had ever had an instant answer to prayer in such an audible way – and while I'd like to tell you it was wonderful and filled me with joy, it actually floored me and left me dumbstruck.

I didn't float through the rest of the day, rather I wandered, almost in a state of shock, going through the motions of my daily routine on the outside, while on the inside I quietly processed what this meant. I never told anyone about that moment, only my now husband and even then it was after we were married. I don't quite know why, perhaps I was afraid of looking silly in case things didn't work out; perhaps I just wanted to keep something special between God and me. Honestly, I don't know the reason. What I do know is that in a very simple way, when I had least expected it and in a very short space of time, God had answered my heart's deepest prayer.

What that simple prayer and simple answer *did* mean was no return trip to Italy. In fact, at the end of my three months I had made the decision to not only stay in New Zealand, but to marry this wonderful man. Yes, dear reader I had become one of those 5-minute-romance-shotgun-wedding gals that I had once eyed so cynically! God's sense of humour was not lost on me then – or now. The world makes you feel older than you really are – and in church years, I was approaching old maid status – however, I found myself at the age of 30 years walking (literally) down the garden path to become the wife of a kind, loving, funny, God-fearing man who was, and still is, my best friend.

I look back on my journey often and think: What will I tell my children when they experience their own season of singleness? I will tell them to hang onto Jesus with all their strength – even if all you have to hold onto is a thread in His garment, even if you only have one finger on the edge of the ledge – hang on to Him because He is hanging on to you.

Waiting is hard, being patient is hard; cleaning up the mess left by the decision not to wait is harder still. Fight for the dreams in your heart and never let them go, hold God to His word and contend for the things He has promised you – God is a good God whose promises are "Yes" and "Amen."

To those of you still waiting for your special someone, encouragement from someone who is on the "other side" can sound trite – and having been where you are I have no desire to add to your heart's weight with fluffy Christianese.

I will simply join my heart with yours, my prayers with yours and my thoughts with yours and walk with you in Spirit until your journey through this season is complete.

Lorinda Frank
Auckland, New Zealand
SunshineForRainyDays.blogspot.com

"When I had least expected it and in a very short space of time, God had answered my heart's deepest prayer."

Irene's Story

*"I really wanted another chance at marriage;
however I didn't believe God would
ever trust me with another one."*

My first marriage ended in my forties, leaving me with a
terrible feeling of guilt. Like I had failed God. I really
wanted another chance at marriage; however I didn't
believe God would ever trust me with another one.

And so twenty-six years went by. (Some of you reading
this – that's your whole lifetime!)

Finally in December 2013, at the age of 71, I told God
that I would do it totally His way if He would give me
another chance. That although it did not look like He was
going to give me a second marriage (at this late stage), I
would be fine with whatever He decided.

I can't say I ever had "a moment" concerning this subject
when I had it out, so to speak, with God. Though I knew
if it was going to happen at all, it would be because of His
blessings on my life.

My daughter and I had shared a townhouse for many
years, but at the beginning of 2014, we decided we would
get our own individual places to live when our lease was
up in July. I would then move to Washington State for a
while, save some money and hopefully move back to
California. While I didn't really want to move out of the
state, I thought it was the right decision at the time and I
was at peace with it.

But in February, *Daniel* asked me out to lunch and I agreed to go. For about two years, Daniel had been going to the same prayer meetings that I attended. We'd spoken (well, made small talk), but that was about it. On our lunch, though, I was surprised by what a good time we had. And so we began to talk more and more, to see each other more and more. I enjoyed spending time with this very thoughtful, kind, and godly man who honors God in all he does.

I fell for him before I realized it! Suddenly I knew I did not want to move to Washington. I realized that I was deeply in love with Daniel and I did not want to leave him. I got to know a wonderful man who was there all that time.

This could only have been God's timing. We had our first date on February 21, 2014 and less than 7 weeks later, we were engaged. Not long after, I went on a 2-week trip, but we talked daily. I missed him so much.

How life can change! Now instead of making plans to move out of the state in July, we were making wedding plans for September! September 6, 2014, to be exact.

Single people from our church, of all ages, were so inspired when they found out I was getting married at the age of 72, that they asked to be invited to the wedding. Some even said, "I had just about given up, but now I believe there is still hope for me!"

Thinking back on my single season, peace came when I decided to let God be God, and when I told Him that He could answer my prayer the way *He* wanted, not the way I thought He should. If He was going to answer with a husband, it would be in His timing. Although I wish I had found that place of peace sooner than I did, I thank God I found it.

I'm also glad I stopped telling God about the kind of man I wanted, because I got exactly who I needed. I truly believe if God had listened to me at the time, I would have missed out on a terrific man!

Now this terrific man and I are still adjusting to each other and it is not always easy. It was not easy in my first marriage either, but God was not included. In this marriage, we are both totally committed to God and to each other. Daniel and I talk and pray together about everything and we try to show patience to one another, relying on God to work in us and in our marriage.

A friend (who has been married for 25 years) told me that in a marriage, you make adjustments daily if you want it to be a good one. My marriage has taught me my need for patience and has shown me that God *is* listening, even when I think He's not, or is not going to answer my prayer. In the end, I know He is going to give me what I need.

I would say, to anyone who is still waiting to be married, don't try to take on God's job, enjoy where you are and above all: "Trust in the Lord with all your heart; do not depend on your own understanding. Seek His will in all you do, and he will show you which path to take." Proverbs 3:5,6 (NLT).

Irene Milks
Van Nuys, California, USA

"God is listening, even when I think He's not. Even when I think He is not going to answer my prayer."

Alisa's Story

"My twenties slipped by, then my thirties.
My fortieth birthday came and went,
and still no husband. "

From the time I was very young all I really wanted to do when I grew up was get married and have babies. I never really aspired to a career, never had a burning desire to work at anything other than taking care of a home and a family. Oh, I didn't sit around waiting for God to bring my man to my door, and I didn't "hunt" for a husband. But I sort of assumed that fairly early on I'd meet him and the rest would be history.

It didn't happen that way.

I graduated from college, went to work, involved myself in my church, and waited for the right man to come into my life. And waited, and waited, and waited. My twenties slipped by, then my thirties. My fortieth birthday came and went, and still no husband. No children. Was I mad at God for not letting my dream come true? Not really. Sad, yes. Many tears were shed.

I think the most aggravating thing well-meaning Christians would say to me during those years was, "But Alisa - singleness is a GIFT." Of course these folks were always married themselves! I'd think, "Really, a gift? You want it? No? I didn't think so!" But (most of the time, anyway) I trusted God to know and to do what was best for me - and I waited, and prayed, and hoped, and waited . . .

Then one day I had an epiphany of sorts. It dawned on me that all this time I had been waiting for my life to happen . . . when in reality this WAS my life. I could either keep on wishing things were different, or get out there and live it. So I surrendered, and told God that my life was his to do with as he pleased, no matter what he asked of me. God's answer was to send me to Oradea, Romania in 2004 (I was 43!) for five of the most wonderful years of my life, working with youth at a small but growing independent church. I learned to live in another culture, learned to love the people, learned to speak Romanian, and learned that I was so much stronger than I ever imagined. And I learned to lean on Jesus like never before. He IS sufficient. He supplied my every need. I could not have been happier, even though I was SINGLE! And no one was more surprised than I was.

In 2009 God made it clear to me that it was time to come home. I returned to the States and moved in with my parents in North Carolina to readjust and figure out what was next. At some point during this time my mother suggested to me that I might want to try eHarmony. My immediate response was NO. I mean, wasn't that "husband-hunting" - something I'd decided I would never do? God didn't need my help to find me a man, and anyway, I was 48 years old and it was getting a little late. Or so I told myself.

My dream of a husband and a family had never really died - I'd just shelved it because it seemed pretty unlikely at that point. But Mom persisted, I prayed, and slowly I came to believe that going online was really just another way of meeting people, people I might not otherwise cross paths with. While this isn't an ad for eHarmony, the important thing is that it was this avenue that God used to finally bring my husband into my life.

David and I started out communicating by email and discovered we had many, many common interests and attitudes about life. He had been married before, and was candid about what had gone wrong and about the fact that he and his first wife had not had a Christ-centered marriage. He had since then fully committed his life to following Jesus and he told me that it was of paramount importance to him that if he ever married again, his wife should be a woman who loved Jesus - and that He be at the center of the marriage.

Emails became long phone conversations and after a few months we decided it was time we met in person. We were at the time living about six hours apart - I was in North Carolina and he was in Maryland - but my parents and I were planning to be in northern Virginia for a few days, so David and I decided to meet in the middle, in Washington, DC. Because we shared a love of museums and history, our first date took place at the Smithsonian Museum of American History - maybe not the most romantic of places, but perfect for us! We were almost instantly comfortable in each other's company and we had a wonderful day together. It was over too soon.

Things progressed, and before too long I was planning a visit to Maryland to go through the acid test - meeting David's two children, who were 12 and 14 years old. We were sure by that time that we wanted to be together and believed that it was God's plan, but it was extremely important to us both that his kids be comfortable with me. And . . . they liked me! It was a key bit of confirmation for us that this really was God's plan and that we belonged together. In addition, I was instantly at home in David's church and with his friends, both our families approved, and in short order we were planning our wedding! We were married on May 22, 2010. I was 49 years old and David was 50.

Has it all been smooth sailing ever since? Well, no. :) I had been single and on my own for a long time, and learning to submit to my husband and share my space was NOT a piece of cake! But it's been so, so worth it. Following God's plan for you always is. I didn't get my family the way I planned when I was young, but my husband and stepchildren are blessings I thank God for each and every day. I wouldn't change a thing now even if I could.

God used my single season to teach me " . . . in whatever state I am, to be content: I know how to be abased, and I know how to abound. Everywhere and in all things I have learned both to be full and to be hungry, both to abound and to suffer need. I can do all things through Christ who strengthens me." (Philippians 4:11-13, NKJV). I wouldn't trade that for the world.

Alisa Dear
Maryland, USA

> *"I could either keep on wishing things were different, or get out there and live my life."*

Deborah's Story

*"I never thought I would get married
with my many mistakes and hurts, and
my poor relationship skills with men."*

After twenty one years of praying for one, God blessed
me with a Christ-centered marriage in 2010 at the age of
52! Yet, it didn't come without some major reconstruction
on my soul. The prolonged preparation launched me into
an unforgettable, no-regrets union with the love of my
life, and a celebration to beat all. It's wonderful when you
wait for God's perfect timing.

Tim and I were both 52 years old and neither of us had
been married before. We both desired marriage for
decades, but God did not introduce us to each other until
we were in our mid forties. Even then, we lived two states
away from each other. How was this ever going to work?
Thankfully, that was not a question we had to answer for
quite some time. God was helping us establish a solid
friendship, and He was doing it in a slow and steady
fashion while He was working out all kinds of issues in
our individual lives.

Tim and I met *virtually* in 2003 on an Internet dating site
that we both joined for only one month! We corresponded
for a year before we met in person for a bike ride in 2004.
Neither of us saw nor felt fireworks at first sight, but we
developed a healthy, pleasing, and loving friendship over
the years. That was something totally new to me with a
man. I was always searching and getting involved too
quickly, only to exit just as quickly at times. Or, I would
stay too long in an unhealthy relationship and not know

how to get out of it. This friendship with a man was new territory for me, and I thrived in it. I remember reading a quote by Ann Landers - *Love is a friendship that has caught fire.* We were collecting kindling for years before that fire was lit between the two of us.

Growing up, unlike so many little girls, I never dreamed of being married someday. My parents fought, drank, and fought some more and eventually divorced when I was 23. Both sets of grandparents were divorced, and both of my sisters went through divorces. I did not want to get divorced! Along with my fear of divorce, I was a mess in my teens and twenties. To put it mildly, I was not marriage material. At my first boy-girl party in 7th grade, five or six guys pinned me down on the ground and began to undress me when a screaming girl sent them scurrying. I was traumatized, and that was the start of my fear and anger toward the male gender, and my subsequent spiral into drinking, drugs, an eating disorder, and promiscuity. Marriage was not among my desires!

But thanks be to God for healing me, and delivering me from all the pain from my past! Given my many mistakes and hurts, and my poor relationship skills with men, I never thought I would get married. Thankfully, through surrendering to the Lord, counseling, lots of reading, joining a twelve-step group, and reading the Bible, I was able to recognize a good man when I finally met one in 2004!

Our early relationship could be compared to a bottle of molasses. We couldn't see through it or into it. It came out ever so slowly, and we had small moments of great sweetness, but it took a long time to pour out. From 2003 to 2007, Tim and I only saw each other five or six times. We kept in touch via email, and maybe a Christmas card or birthday phone call (since we are only 15 days apart in age). We were both looking for companionship, and I had serious relationships with two men that ended poorly in 2004 and 2007. Tim was my friend through those relationships, and I respected his male insights and perspectives. He was a faithful friend during those "early years" of our relationship.

Then came Father's Day of 2007. I was waitressing (my second job to help me get out of debt). Tim had come to Massachusetts to visit a high school friend that weekend. He asked me if I wanted to do one of three things before he drove back to Maine: he could come over and help me with my finances (he is a CPA), we could go for a bike ride (but I had worked double shifts all weekend), or we could go to a concert. The Selah concert won out and when he went to leave that night, we hugged goodbye. I remember being in his arms for the first time, and not wanting to let go! God was stirring up feelings in me that took me completely by surprise! It happened again when we met in December of 2007 to celebrate our fiftieth birthdays together.

Our friendship was catching a few more sparks in 2008 when Tim invited me to visit Acadia National Park for a few days in July. We met again in September for a 100-mile bike ride in New Hampshire. At a Sunday church service, we sat next to a woman who, when she discovered we were just friends, said, "Why aren't you two married? You are both so good looking!" We laughed, but I was beginning to wonder whether we would someday be more than friends. My sister and dad met Tim when they came to visit in October of 2008. My sister told me later that she thought we would be married someday. I'm not sure where she got that idea from. After all, he had never even kissed me!

Well, that finally changed in January of 2009. Now that we were visiting more often, hotel bills were accumulating. God is very clear in His Word that we are to remain pure until marriage. My past relationships did not follow that rule, but this one with Tim would and did. After we attended church and went out for lunch, I went back to his apartment, and before I headed south, he kissed me! I was shocked and amazed, and so giddy, I got on the phone as soon as I pulled out of his parking lot and called my sister!

Shortly, I wanted the D.T.R. - *Define the Relationship* talk. Tim wouldn't define it! I was frustrated, but needed to seek the Lord and wait on Him. My sister kept on telling me to shut up and not bring that up anymore! She said Tim was smitten with me and I had nothing to worry about. Her advice was to just enjoy him and let things go. Keeping my mouth shut was difficult, especially since I had no idea where our relationship was going. As far as I knew, he still had an open account on eHarmony!

I waited another *twenty months* before Tim finally proposed on the top of Cadillac Mountain in April 2010. Since we knew each other for so many years, and we were 52, we decided to marry two days after my school year was finished, approximately eight weeks after he proposed. Tim retired from his long-term corporate job and became our official wedding planner. We had much to do: premarital counseling, and all the plans that go into creating a beautiful wedding day.

Shortly after Tim proposed, while still atop Cadillac Mountain in Acadia National Park, we decided to bicycle across the country together on our honeymoon! So, in addition to planning a wedding, we planned a self-supported bicycle trip across the country, a dream we both had even before we met.

The bike trip accelerated our marital bonding. If our courtship was compared to a bottle of molasses, the bike trip made our marriage like a delicious soda on a hot summer day, with lots of fizz and so satisfying after years of thirsting for a partner. We went from single and solitary living to 24/7 togetherness. We had a goal and a dream together to bicycle across America, and together we did it. We fell more deeply in love with the Lord and each other during that trip. We were on the road from July 1st, less than two weeks after walking down the aisle, until September 1st of 2010. That was a lot of time together - and we relished in it!

God led Tim and me to write a book about our experience on the road and the first two months of our marriage. We titled the book: *Two are Better: Midlife Newlyweds Bicycle Coast to Coast*. In it, we share the many blessings, as well as the lessons the Lord has taught us after waiting so long for love. I can't emphasize enough the importance of waiting for the right person. Sharing the same faith is crucial to having a healthy marriage. Every night, Tim and I pray and read the Bible together. There have been times when I have been so angry and unloving towards him. But, when we come together to pray and read the Bible, God convicts me of my sin, and softens my heart.

Back in 1996, I moved east after living in Colorado for twenty years. I quit my teaching job and returned to the East Coast to be closer to my family. I remember praying to the Lord on my long trek across country, and felt like He said, *"Your husband is on the East Coast."* I held onto that promise for *fourteen years*. Most people would think that was crazy to wait that long, but I knew in my heart that the Lord would deliver on His promise.

Waiting on the Lord is the key to a happy life, and a happy marriage. I spent too many years running the show, getting into messes, and learning the hard way. God knew I wasn't ready for marriage when I first asked Him for a husband back in 1989. He worked on me for 21 years to shape me into "marriage material." He loved me through all my doubts and insecurities. Being married doesn't erase all my faults and character defects. Actually, it tends to bring them into the spotlight at times. But the beauty of our relationship comes from the Bible: *A cord of three strands is not easily broken.* When I hold onto my Lord, and walk with my husband in a desire to live a life worthy of God's calling, everyday becomes an adventure in Holy Matrimony!

Deborah Lee Bishop
Marlborough, Massachusetts, USA
www.openroadpress.com

> *"I knew in my heart that the Lord would deliver on His promise."*

Lori's Story

"While I was trying to become the
perfect old maid, I was also pursuing
one bad relationship after another."

My single season was terrible. I grew up in a very conservative Christian environment, so marriage was part of the air I breathed. It was the next logical step in your life. Grow up, go to college, get married. I remember at the age of 26 feeling like a complete and utter failure because I hadn't gotten married yet.

Because I didn't want to be thought of as a failure, I decided to become an "old maid missionary." After all, didn't Paul say in 1 Corinthians that if you're single you should focus on serving the Lord? And that seemed to be the only acceptable way for a single woman to shed the stigma of being single. I spent several years applying to missions organizations and failing. But I don't remember getting angry at God (I was so busy trying to compensate for my "failure" that I didn't really think to be angry.). To quote Thoreau, I was living a "life of quiet desperation."

I attended a large church with an active single's group. Our Sunday School teacher, however, was "old school": found his sweetheart at Bible College, served in ministry together for a long time, etc. So, bless their hearts, he and his wife couldn't really relate to us. Once he told us we should be more active in the church, and boy did that touch a nerve!

I remember one lady saying she had told the youth pastor she would love to help out with the teens. According to her, she was actually told that the church didn't want singles working with the youth because "it would set a bad example." That was a real eye-opener. It was the first time I heard any bias against singles, at least in Christian circles. (If you're in a church where you don't feel welcome because you're single, then run. There are other churches.)

After my last, failed attempt to become a missionary, my mother sat down with me. She told me I should stop wasting my time. Go find your dream job, she said. Enjoy your life. When God is ready for you to get married or become a missionary or whatever, He'll know where to find you. After that I felt much more at peace. I took her advice and poured myself into a job I loved. That gave me some breathing time to heal and get to know myself better.

I learned that I was a lot stronger than I thought. After I stopped being desperate, I moved several states for that great job my mother encouraged me to find. Once there, I plugged into another church with another active single's group. This church, though, embraced their singles, so I learned I could enjoy myself and be fulfilled without being married. I learned that God cares about *us*, too.

My mom was right—of course! God loved me even when I wasn't a saint living in a mud hut overseas somewhere. He loved me right there in Denver, Colorado doing a totally secular job. And I know it's a cliché, but it is so true: His timing is so much better! If I had married one of those other guys, I know I would have added the heartbreak of divorce to my other pain.

In the meantime, I signed up for one of those online dating sites. A year went past and nothing happened, so I actually forgot I had joined. Then one night I got an e-mail from some guy in Britain. I was going through a very stressful time then - my car had been totaled in an accident, so I was wrestling with the insurance, the garage, not to mention finding a way to work. Anyway, without thinking, I deleted his e-mail. A month later, he tried again. This time I wrote back and the rest was history.

This was absolutely a dream come true for me. Since I was a little girl, I had loved Great Britain. I could go on forever, but suffice it to say that Mr. Right for me was the modern equivalent of Mr. Darcy. And now here he was writing to me!

I was 31 when I met Andrew and we got married a year later. He was 42. Neither one of us had ever been married before.

Andrew told me he had been praying for a wife for quite a while. He felt the Lord telling him she could come from a great distance. He thought God meant from across England! However, he decided to give me a chance, and here we are ten years later. I knew he was the One when I flew over to meet him. He had just returned from a vacation in Holland and gave me a pair of miniature wooden shoes "for your little dainty feet." (I'm only 5'2".) I nearly cried. All of my life I had been clumsy, the proverbial last one chosen for a team sport on the playground. Now, here was this man I had known for only a month calling me delicate. I knew I'd accept if he ever proposed.

I am so glad I was older when I got married. Honestly, my life was a mess earlier. I talked above about trying to compensate by becoming a missionary. Well, I actually had a kind of schizophrenic existence. While I was trying to become the perfect old maid, I was also pursuing one bad relationship after another. I would be friends with a guy, think I had fallen in love with him, then get my hopes up, only to have them dashed.

Also, since Andrew and I had spent so many years waiting, it didn't take forever to decide whether we were "right" or not. We both were in a place where we wanted to get married, so we didn't have a bunch of hemming and hawing trying to decide "what the status of our relationship was."

I can't speak for every couple, but we really didn't have an issue about merging our lives. I moved over to England when we got married, so obviously I had to be very flexible. And Andrew is such a nice person, he's like, "Ok, whatever. It's all good." So we just fit together like a pair of shoes.

If I could go back and shake my single self, I would say so many things. First and foremost, DON'T judge yourself because you don't have a ring on your finger. Know and believe that God loves you just as you are.

I don't know why, but I noticed that the men in my church singles' groups never ended up marrying the women in the group. They always found love outside of the group. So don't be desperate, constantly waiting for some guy friend to become the One. It's exhausting, and totally unfair to the men in your life. If all they want is friendship, then fine. Enjoy it. And be open to finding your guy somewhere else.

DON'T gloss over warning signs in a relationship. I cannot emphasize this enough. Looking back, I can see how God protected me. I made some bad relationship choices, and thank God, they didn't work out. That was not before I suffered heartache, though, because deep down I knew they were unhealthy relationships. I was just so desperate that I pretended I could make them work.

Find something to do with yourself that you really like. It doesn't have to be a job. Join a class at your community college and learn something new. Save up and travel to a place you've always wanted to see. Before I met Andrew, I actually traveled to Britain on my own just because I wanted to. It was easier to do it back when I was single. I had total freedom to do what I wanted, and it sure cost a lot less than traveling with two people.

If you go the online route, then be honest in your profile. By the time I put mine up, I thought I had nothing to lose, so why not? I talked frankly about how I loved sports. Turns out that was the first thing that attracted Andrew to me! Actually, I guess that applies for face-to-face relationships, too. Don't make yourself miserable trying to be something you're not.

Lori Buckle
Dallas, Texas, USA
www.luxdomine.com

> *"I know it's a cliché, but it is so true:*
> *His timing is so much better! If I had*
> *married one of those other guys, I know*
> *I would have added the heartbreak*
> *of divorce to my other pain."*

Theresa's Story

"When my husband left me for another woman,
I thought I would just remain single."

I met my first husband at age eighteen and was married at
the young age of twenty. I really didn't know anything
about dating nor had I ever been intimate with another
man. Therefore, when my husband left me for another
woman, I thought I would just remain single. As I
mention in my book, the mere thought of being intimate
with someone else was beyond my ability to comprehend.

I'm sure those of you who are divorced or those of you
who may be going through a divorce can relate to the
pain.

Is there life after divorce? I can boldly proclaim to you,
"Yes, there is!" However, I was not always able to answer
this with such confidence.

I was thankful that I had an intimate relationship with The
Lord. My walk with Jesus brought me through. The Holy
Spirit was there, comforting me and letting me know that
God had a good future and good plans for me.

During the six years of my alone season, I was content to
dwell. I was at peace with my decision to remain single. I
grew strong; I became whole again. I actually enjoyed this
new independent me. I had even decided to go on a
church cruise! While packing for the trip, I prayed a
prayer which I did not intend to pray; I prayed for God to
send me "an usher."

That's when my life made a dramatic shift.

A prophet of God happened to join us on the cruise. At a farewell meeting the night before it ended, he shared that God showed him "companionships" coming to the single women. He mentioned the following year, at about the same time, there would be weddings. The cruise took place in February 2005.

When I heard this news I slapped my friend, Ann, on the arm saying, "I'm getting married next year!" She laughed. I seriously thought I was kidding because I had forgotten the prayer I prayed a week before this prophecy came forth!

The very next Sunday, I attended church and proceeded to sit where I always did. But a new usher led me to my seat.

I honestly didn't remember the prayer, or the prophecy. Becoming married was not really at the top of my "to-do," list. However, now I was open to the thought of marriage. My thinking had changed. Time often has the ability to allow us to see differently. At this point, I wouldn't have minded meeting someone, but none of this was registering. I figured the usher who was usually in the section where I sat, year in and year out, was sick or on vacation, but not so. He was mysteriously assigned to another section.

This newly-assigned usher, Roy, was 52 and I was actually a month shy of turning 53 when we met. And as the weeks went on, Roy and I would talk. I was shy. The first time he complimented me, I ran out of the church blushing! This caused him to back off and slow down. He slowed down so much though, I had to ask him to come to a family dinner (or I might still be waiting for a date right now!). Even after the dinner, it took him some time. And I kept thinking, "Come on now, I am not a spring chicken!"

It wasn't long after meeting Roy that God revealed to me he was the one. I knew in my "knower" that God had supernaturally placed him there, sitting next to me in church, in order for us to meet. Prior to that day, I had never seen him and he had never seen me, even though we both attended the same church for years. I believe God kept us from each other until we were both ready. Roy, too, prayed a similar prayer, asking God to send him a wife around the same time I had prayed for God to send me "an usher." But Roy still was not sure if marriage was on the top of his list. He was more afraid than I was!

Even so, Roy became my husband the following March of 2006. We married when Roy was 53 and I was 54 (As Roy is eight months younger than I am, he calls me the older woman!). At these ages we had come to the conclusion that since we knew this was God ordained, "Why wait?" While we both were (and still are) believing God for long, healthy lives, life is short and after living a half-century, well, let's get on with the show!

Sometimes I think we had better watch out what we pray for! I asked for "an usher?" Wherever did that come from except the mind of God?

At our ages, we were indeed set in our ways. We each had slept in a queen bed separately for so long. When we were first married, we attempted to sleep in a queen-size bed together, but in a matter of weeks, we went out and bought king-size mattresses!

Then there are the family members to adjust to. God never intended that families split up. So, although God blesses and restores lives, families take time to adjust. In our case, we had my dad whom I was caring for. Roy had agreed to continue to take care of Dad, but when we were married for only three months, my daughter came knocking on our door with four small children seeking refuge from a bad marriage. It was difficult to say the least!

This second marriage has taught me, "The grass is not greener on the other side." We learn to love sacrificially as we allow someone to rub against our grain. And this goes for good marriages. It is difficult for two people to come together as one; difficult yes, but possible because of Jesus.

It is also vital for Christians to understand God's love for them. It is only then that we can love God in return, ourselves, others, and of course our spouses. Human love doesn't cut it. When I comprehend how much God loves me, how can I not give my all to my husband, even when I feel I am wronged? This mindset will cause any marriage to prosper and enable good marriages to become better!

I would encourage anyone desiring to be married that you desire a good thing! Set your heart on Jesus and be content to dwell there. Pray, put your order in, and then rest in Him. Father God takes pleasure in giving you the desires of your heart. Wait patiently on Him.

Remember, in every situation, Jesus will cause light to shine out from the darkness. He will always bring us into a fruitful place. When in Christ, our pain will always turn into our gain; it's Kingdom life!

Theresa Wolmart
Florida, USA
Google.com/+TheresaWolmart

> *"I grew strong; I became whole again. My thinking had changed. Time often has the ability to allow us to see differently."*

Francine's Story

"I swore that I'd never love again."

I was forty something when I finally divorced and I swore that I'd never love or marry again. I decided I'll gracefully grow old alone.

Shortly after my divorce, I relocated from New Jersey to Georgia with my job. I worked hard on recovering, recuperating, rearranging and reorganizing my life in my new home state. I didn't have time for dating, nor was I in that frame of mind. I also chose to ignore the handsome man that kept trying to pursue me. Every chance he got, he asked me out and every chance I got, I politely turned him down. I was perfectly contented.

Three years had passed, he remained the same, but by this time, I was the one who was beginning to change. I was now in my mid-forties, my broken heart had healed and I was ready to start dating. And to be perfectly honest, I had begun to pray about a mate and a companion. Even though I had accepted my singleness, this time I wasn't going to take matters of the heart into my own hands. I knew if I were to be given a second chance at love and marriage, this time, I'd leave it up to God, His choice, His timing, His plans and His will, not mine.

I began to wait and hope that if the unwavering handsome man would ask me out again, I decided I was going to say, "Yes."

One day he asked me if I would like to go fishing with him. I thought to myself, "Wow, just when I make up my mind to say, 'Yes,' he asks me to go fishing; I would've preferred him asking me out to dinner, rather than catching it." However, I smiled and said, "Yes, I'd like that." I prepared a nice picnic lunch and we went to a picturesque park where among nature's most beautiful settings, he patiently taught me how to fish.

At the end of the day and with our last worm, I caught my very first fish. He then took me to meet his family before stopping by a taxidermist to have my tiny brim stuffed and mounted. It was a date filled with fun, laughter and good conversation. It also turned out to be the most romantic first date I ever had and we didn't even kiss. On the way home, I couldn't help but to wonder if this was a sign of answered prayer.

A few years later, I was diagnosed with breast cancer and I was so thankful for his love, attentiveness and support. Being so far from my home and family, God supplied my needs at that time which included him. However, as the years passed and as close as we were and as much as we needed and were there for each other, neither one of us ever talked about marriage. The subject seemed to be taboo. He was a confirmed bachelor and I was contented with the way things were. The thought of marriage was frightening for two independent, self-sufficient, middle-aged people who were set in their ways, but we knew in our hearts that after almost nine years of dating, it was the right thing to do. Besides, we knew marriage was honorable and the marriage bed undefiled.

New Year's Eve 2008, we came in from church; he poured us some champagne and got on one knee. I really thought he was looking for something, so I told him to get up before he couldn't! (Remember, we're at the ages where we don't do any unnecessary bending and kneeling.) He took out a black velvet box and asked me to be his wife, but before I could say "Yes," he had gotten up and sat on the couch next to me, laughingly saying, "I tried to be romantic, but I have to do this sitting down." We hugged, kissed and toasted, and in that hug and kiss, we both knew the answer.

A year passed without us thinking much about marriage or making any kind of wedding plans. On February 1, 2009, he said, "Hey, Valentine's Day is on Saturday this year; let's get married." Surprised, I jokingly said, "What's the hurry?" He said, "Do you remember when you had your first Chemotherapy treatment?" I said, "Yeah, it was on Valentine's Day." He said, "Ever since then, Valentines Day has never been the same for you. I want it to be a day you can love and cherish, instead of it always reminding you of chemo, cancer and sickness. I promised you back then that if you could just get through that time, I'd give you a Valentines Day you'll never forget, one that'll make you happy and as much as I tried, I could never figure out that extra special something to do. I want to be a man of my word and I want us to get married on that day."

We decided on a small intimate house wedding with immediate family and friends. For the next two weeks, I ran around like a chicken without a head looking for the perfect dress, shoes, cake and decorations and planning a menu. Most of the time was spent looking for something to wear. Two days before the wedding, I was simply worn out and still hadn't found my dress or shoes. With tears in my eyes and almost on the verge of calling it off, I decided to give it one more try. At the very last minute, I found the perfect outfit and everything started to fall perfectly in line.

My husband and everybody else cried as he read his vows. My bouquet was off white roses with a red one in the center, which I placed in front of my mother's picture in memory of her since she had recently passed. I also gave a rose to each person who had a special meaning to me. Since everyone was old, already married or too young to think about it, there was no need in tossing the bouquet. There were well wishes as we toasted, ate and danced our first dance as husband and wife amidst iridescent bubbles. It turned out to be an absolutely beautiful, blessed day.

We couldn't stop talking and thinking about the day as my husband and I slowly drifted off to sleep in each other's arms. My husband was right, Valentine's Day will always be a day I will remember, not for the illness, the Chemo and the pain, but for the love, the happiness, the wonderful memories and also as our anniversary.

Since then, it hasn't been as easy as we thought it would be. Dating and living in separate houses is totally different from marriage and living under one roof; I don't care how well you think you know each other or how long you've dated. It takes constant prayer, faith, understanding, respect, communication, patience, honesty, sincerity, trust in God and a desire, determination and sense of commitment for a marriage to work. It also takes doing the same things that brought you together to keep you together. Gracefully growing older together means that's its imperative to be mindful and realistic of each other's expectations and responsibilities, as well as physical and mental capabilities.

Even though we're now in our young sixties, the fact of the matter is that we are in our sixties and health issues, aches, pains, fatigue and forgetting comes naturally and can become challenging and problematical for recently married middle aged couples. However, God ordained marriage and He will stand behind His word. He will give you the strength and the wisdom to work out your problems (and there will be problems), but both have to be willing to work them out. Marriage is a union of two people. It is not one-sided and you are not alone in it. He is in the midst of it.

God really does answer prayers! He will put you and your mate in each other's paths at the right time and at the right place, and He will give you who and what you need when you need it. Read His word. Believe His word. Stand on His word and confess it as a single person believing Him for a mate. Let Him lead and guide you, because with Him all things really are possible.

Francine Billingslea
Lithonia, Georgia, USA

*"God really does answer prayers!
With Him all things really are possible."*

Melissa's Story

*"I'm sure there's a giant warehouse
in Heaven filled from ceiling to
cellar with bottles of my tears."*

From a very young age, I was in love with love. Romance. Fairy tales. The "Happy Ending Kiss." Growing up, I dreamt of finding my true love some day, but I never really believed anyone would ever want *me*. I knew I wasn't pretty. I definitely wasn't popular. If a guy ever *was* interested, I was only ever a "one date wonder" when they discovered I wouldn't sleep with them before marriage.

My first kiss was as a young teenager at a church summer camp. He was a 17 year old, tanned, very fit, *scoundrel* who captivated me with a swoon-worthy smooch (picture Scarlett and Rhett) by the cafeteria and then moments later (while I was still in a semi-conscious daze), he was lip-locked with someone else behind the snack shop. But I didn't care. He noticed me. He was good looking and he must've thought I was something special - even for a moment. And a moment was good enough for me.

Thus began a long period of making excuses for the other scoundrels that came across my path. I didn't think I was worth any more than the scraps of attention I was thrown.

At the ripe old age of 19, I entered into a disastrous marriage. No amount of warning from worried onlookers would dissuade me from walking down that aisle. And when I finally had the courage to leave, I'd blown through the better part of my 20's. Never one to do things by halves, I did what any romantic, freedom-seeking adventurer on an epic quest would do. I left Los Angeles for a kingdom, far, far away. The United Kingdom, to be exact. After more than four years, God then moved me on to New Zealand.

Though my country hopping yielded amazing experiences and lifelong heart friendships, it was also filled with years of dating, waiting and heart-rending disappointment. A long term relationship, that tossed me to and fro as I waited three years for it to turn into marriage, ultimately left me shipwrecked in a distant land. Years later, another attachment was severed as I bid farewell to yet another country.

I was beginning to get the feeling that it was SO important for me to end up with the right guy, God would completely uproot me and send me halfway around the world just so I wouldn't end up with the wrong guy ever again. Nevertheless, my heart felt pretty bruised.

In the spring of 2012, it was back to America. Not to Los Angeles where I still had some sort of community, but up to Washington where my Dad lived and where I had no friends, no job, no church . . . Just sadness.

Though I'm sure there's a giant warehouse in Heaven filled from ceiling to cellar with bottles of my tears, somehow I didn't give in to unbelief. Somehow, I clung to hope and to my certainty of God's goodness. Even when family members tried to persuade me that maybe the single life was what God had for me, that maybe there actually *wasn't* someone for me and I should *probably* make peace with that, I knew; I KNEW I was meant to find love somewhere. I knew that I would be married to the right guy some day. So I kept putting myself out there.

With a lot of reading and research into heartbreak mending, relationships, commitment issues, and how guys think; and with a lot of journaling, praying, crying and Skyping things out with girlfriends, God took me on a brave, internal journey of healing and growth. One to match the grand scope of my international travels.

All the while I was praying for my future husband. Not just that God would bring him, (and this is key) but thanking God that he existed and actually praying *for* him – for his day, his health, his finances, his dreams, etc. I declared Scripture over myself and over him and never let a negative confession pass through my lips that he wasn't out there or that I'd never get married. I just kept thanking God for my future husband and speaking out loud that he was on his way! Your words have power, you know.

In that summer of 2012, as I was in between countries, my prayers for my future husband went up a notch. I felt God lead me to pray specific things and in earnest for him. I'd always had strong feelings that my husband was not American (and most probably British, but most probably *not* a New Zealander), and that summer, I just knew that he was far away and must be going through something difficult as I was urged to pray for things like healing from disappointment and heartache and to declare favour, peace, hope and strength over him.

It was also at that time the idea for this book came to me. I was so excited about it, I couldn't sleep. However, I felt God say that the timing for it wasn't right, so I reluctantly put it to the side.

Meanwhile an opportunity to go back to the UK for a short while opened up to me at the beginning of 2013 and off I was again. Though I spent time with a couple of guys, my husband wasn't there either.

But God was moving things behind the scenes. While I was in England, a job offer came from my church back in New Zealand. Would I consider returning? Even though I'd received unfulfilled prophetic words about New Zealand being my "country of breakthrough," since I had to leave the life I'd built there, I figured they must've been wrong. I thought that book was closed forever.

Nevertheless, I sensed God repositioning me, so on the last day of July, 2013, I was off again . . .

Shane and I met at church a few months later after a Sunday night service. He seemed to not really know anyone, so I introduced myself and sought to get him connected with the rest of the 20's-30's group while I was busy gathering them all up for pizza and movies at the house. Feeling new again to the church myself, I was meeting lots of people and didn't think much of it.

(Besides, I was going on dates with other guys I met when I arrived in New Zealand and I would find out later that Shane was busy working through the rubble of a failed marriage a year and a half prior. Not the most ideal timing.)

It was also that week, at the end of October 2013, that God brought this book project back to mind and told me it was time to get to work. As 2014 came into view, I kept seeing it, not as 2014, but as 214. As in 2/14. As in February 14. As in Valentine's Day. As in Love. I had a strong feeling that 2014 was the "Year of Love." But since there was nobody around that could've been a potential, I wondered if it was just my imagination.

In the months that followed though, Shane and I became good friends. He challenged me about going on regular outings with someone who was more than a friend, but less than a boyfriend, especially when I knew there was no future there. And because of my own experience with an ill-fated marriage, I helped him sort through his thoughts and feelings about what he had gone through.

As time passed, although I believed he saw me only as a friend, or as a sister even, the friendship started to blossom into more than that. Meanwhile God knew that because of all I'd been through (and the difficulties we would encounter getting to the altar!), I needed beyond-a-doubt, Holy Spirit confirmation that He was in this.

And did the confirmation come! Fast and furious. Before and after Shane declared that he had feelings for me, the prophetic words poured in – from the very young to the very old, from strangers and friends alike who "didn't know anything about anything." Heaven being so vocal was definitely exciting!

And when I looked back at my "list," (yes, I broke down and made one) and saw that Shane was all the things I was believing for (and more), like passionate about God and the supernatural, creative, smart, good looking, supportive, adventurous and fun, and even seemingly frivolous things like believing he would be British (in addition to being a New Zealander [God's sense of humour - never say never!], he also has British citizenship), there was NO mistaking that God brought us together. It was also fun to realize that the first day I ever set foot on New Zealand soil also happened to be his birthday. Happy birthday to him!

We got engaged the weekend that marked my one year anniversary of being back in New Zealand and we married exactly 2 months later on the evening of the 3rd of October. Walking down a candle lit, twisty, curving aisle (opposed to the traditional straight aisle) was the perfect symbolic demonstration of the meandering path I had walked to find my husband at the end of it.

Now we thought we picked the date and time because we wanted a night wedding and time enough to fly from Auckland to Paris to arrive on Shane's birthday. But we discovered, after the wedding, that the 3rd of October was not only the day I left America for New Zealand for the first time (to embark on another adventure into the unknown), but it is German Reunification Day AND this year (2014), at sundown it marked the beginning of Yom Kippur, a day of restoration. Setting off on a new adventure. Restoration and reunification. A powerful summation for both of us!

Before I met Shane, I never had a grid for how easy being with someone could be. How happy and loved and supported I could feel. I held onto this faith, this hope that I hadn't had the experience of, but *somehow* knew existed for me. Just like in Hebrews 11:1: "Now faith is the substance of things hoped for, the evidence of things not seen." (NKJV)

No matter what had happened to me, or what anyone else said, love *was* out there. And now from a fellow sister who persevered, I'm joining my heart with yours in thanking God for your husband because I believe love is out there for you, too.

Be encouraged!

Melissa Williams Pope
Auckland, New Zealand (by way of the UK, by way
of the USA)
www.LoveisOutThere.com

> *"I just kept thanking God for my
> future husband and all the while
> I was praying for him."*

Your Turn: Share Your Story

Did you, or someone you know, find love and marriage later in life? Would you like to be featured on the *Love is Out There* blog or in a possible Volume II of the book?

I'm looking for fresh stories to continue to encourage the thousands of single Christian women still waiting for God to reveal their husbands - yours could be one of them!

(If you'd like to share your story, but aren't sure how to write it, my friend Bobbie loves to help others share their testimonies, and you can download her free Story Structure Success Sheet at testimonytrain.com.)

Ready to send in your story of hope?
Just go to: www.LoveisOutThere.com/Share

What's Next?

You didn't think I'd leave you hanging, did you? No way! That's why I've created these two sample prayers for you, as well as the 21-Day Heart Exploration Experience for your private journaling and prayer times.

You can also use this 21-Day Experience section for your own *Love is Out There* Heart Exploration group. You'll be amazed at the difference surrounding yourself with supportive friends on the same journey can make!

Prayer for Yourself

Dear God,

Thank you that you love me and that you have a good plan for my life. Thank you that you are leading and guiding me, and directing all of my steps.

You know me better than anyone ever could, for you created me. When I'm feeling lonely, help me to feel your comfort. When I'm faced with decisions, help me to hear your voice.

Thank you that you know all of the desires of my heart regarding every facet of life, even the ones that I've never dared to share with anyone. God, I want to be married. You already know this is a desire of my heart. I ask that, in your timing, you open my eyes to the one you've set aside for me and that you open his eyes to me. I trust that you do have perfect timing and I know that when I look back on this single season, I'll understand why the wait was so long. You're a good Father and I believe you have the very best in store for me. Help me, God, in the moments I find it hard to believe that.

I want to avoid making heart-sick choices as I wait for him.

Thank you for walking with me during this time, for all of the joy you put in my life, the people that you've surrounded me with and all of the blessings you have given me.

Thank you for helping me when I feel afraid or angry or disappointed to continually put my faith and hope and trust in your goodness and your love for me.

Even though I can't see and don't understand what you're doing right now, I choose to trust you and accept your peace. I'm excited to see what the future holds!

Prayer for Your Future Husband

Dear God,

Thank you for my future husband. Thank you that he exists and that whether I know him right now or not, you will reveal him at the exact right time.

I thank you that he is a good man, who loves you with all of his heart and that you're preparing him, even now, right where he is, to be the husband who will be perfect for me – just as you're preparing me to be what he needs, too.

I ask, God, that you heal his mind and heart from any experiences or pain that he could be dealing with right now. That you show him how loved he is by you and how you have wonderful plans for his life. Give him hope, God, that I'm out here. Encourage him that he will find me in your perfect timing. Help him to avoid making heart-sick choices as he waits for me.

I pray now, God, that you give him a wonderful day today and that you pour your blessings of peace, health, financial provision, favour and joy out on him right at this very moment, whatever he's doing and wherever in the world he is . . .

21-Day Heart Exploration Experience

Day 1: Which stories gave you the most encouragement, spoke to you or resonated with you? Why?

Day 2: If you could meet with any of the ladies featured in this book, who would it be and why?

Day 3: After reading the stories, what steps do you feel God might be nudging you towards?

Day 4: Which friend, group of friends or family members could you ask to join with you in regular prayer for your future husband? What day will you start praying together?

Day 5: Is there room in your life (and your heart!) right now for God to bring someone to you? Explore this.

Day 6: What qualities, for you, make a man good "marriage material"?

Day 7: What frightens you the most about being single? Now imagine that God is writing you a letter about this. What does He say? Who do you need Him to be for you right now?

Day 8: Come up with at least ten positive declarations, affirmations or encouraging sentences about yourself. For example: I am worthy of love. I continually walk in God's favour. I make an award winning red velvet cake. Anything! How easy or difficult was that? Why?

Day 9: What belief or habit might God be asking you to let go of right now? Will you? Why or why not?

Day 10: How easy do you find the act of receiving? It could be money, help of any kind or an unexpected gift. Explore what that brings up for you.

Day 11: For fun, imagine it's 40 years in the future and you're looking back on how you met your husband. Write five whacky scenarios and be as detailed and creative as you like. Now read them over again and describe what these mini stories could be saying to you.

Day 12: Where does your heart need healing today?

Day 13: What five things are you most looking forward to being able to bring to a relationship?

Day 14: It is said that the media gives us unrealistic expectations of men and relationships. How have your hopes for and ideas of marriage been affected by novels, films and television shows? Give examples.

Day 15: Craft your own prayer for your future husband. Are there specific things you feel led to pray for him about right now?

Day 16: Think of your previous romantic relationships or relationships you've observed. List five things you've learned about them regarding what you would love to experience in your future.

Day 17: Think again of your previous romantic relationships or relationships you've observed. List five things you've learned about them regarding what you will not accept or tolerate in a relationship.

Day 18: Hindsight can be a really comforting thing. When

you look back on times that a relationship you've had didn't work out, or the guy you were interested in (or loved) didn't return your feelings, are you able to see good reasons why? Explain.

Day 19: What negative things have been spoken to you by others about your likelihood or your desires to be married? List them out and then next to each one, refute them with a positive response.

Day 20: What negative thoughts have you had or negative things have you said to yourself or others about your likelihood or your desires to be married? List them out and then next to each one, refute them with a positive response.

Day 21: Now after reading this book and exploring the above questions, what conclusions can you draw about what you've discovered or explored during this process?

Thank You and a Request

Dear Friend,

Thank you so much for reading through this book and going on the journey! If you enjoyed Love is Out There, *would you please take a moment to visit the site you purchased this book on and leave a review? That will help others looking for encouragement and hope regarding this topic find it more easily. Thank you!*

Believing with you,
Melissa

About Melissa

Melissa Williams Pope can't resist a good love story and seeing dreams come true! Originally from Los Angeles, Melissa holds advanced degrees in pastoral ministry and classical acting, and is a freelance writer, actor, singer and former church staffer.

When not glued to her laptop or memorizing lines, she can also be found coaching or delivering creative dream fulfillment workshops. And even though she spent about a decade crisscrossing the globe from Europe to the South Pacific, Mr Right still miraculously found her! She currently gets to enjoy living the newlywed life with him in Auckland, New Zealand.

She invites you to connect with her at:
www.LoveisOutThere.com
www.TheBusyQuill.com

CPSIA information can be obtained
at www.ICGtesting.com
Printed in the USA
LVOW10s0308101017
551850LV00026B/1273/P